Ron Phillips has written an inspired and moving treatise concerning the often-misunderstood subject of spiritual beings and forces. My encouragement is that every believer will benefit from this book and those who are questioning the presence and relevance of spiritual forces will have their questions answered.

—TOMMY BARNETT
Pastor, Phoenix First Assembly
Dream Centers: Phoenix, Los Angeles, New York

A story has been told of how the first Russian cosmonaut, Yuri Gagarin, was instructed by Soviet premier Nikita Khrushchev to watch out for angels when he went into space in April 1962. On his return he reported that he had not seen any. Khrushchev is said to have replied, "Good, I knew you wouldn't. There is no such thing!" As Christians whose manual of truth is the Bible, we know angels do exist and that they have always played a major role in the history of man from the beginning. Pastor Ron Phillips, in his new book *Our Invisible Allies*, has done a masterful job of providing us with an incredible overview of these special messengers God uses in unique ways and for various purposes.

—MARCUS D. LAMB
President and CEO, Daystar Television Network

Pastor Ron Phillips has been our friend for years, and I have admired him and been blessed by his television broadcasts and his love and concern for people. A great Bible teacher and a man of love and compassion, Ron is a remarkable man of God. If you will read *Our Invisible Allies*, it will help you to know that God loves you, He wants the very best for you, and He desires to grant you the desires of your heart.

—DODIE OSTEEN
Cofounder, Lakewood Church

If you have ever survived a car accident, returned from a battlefield without harm, escaped danger moments before it struck, or avoided an accident by a few seconds, then you may have been assisted by an invisible yet very real force.

Every day the Almighty has commissioned invisible allies to assist the lives of those who are in covenant with Him. While we may never see these angelic forces with our natural eyes, they are nonetheless present and are sent forth to minister to the heirs of salvation.

In Ron Phillips's landmark book *Our Invisible Allies*, this dynamic pastor, teacher, and scholar of the Word of God will open the Scriptures and detail for you what God wants you to know about angels and their mission to minister to you. This book is filled with unique faith-building stories and is easy to understand, even for those who are young in the faith.

It is my joy to recommend this book to all believers who want to learn more about the spiritual world and the angels who help direct it.

—PERRY STONE JR.
Voice of Evangelism Ministries Inc. and
Host of *Manna-fest*

Our Invisible Allies by Ron Phillips takes you on a fascinating journey into the realm of the supernatural. He lifts the veil between the seen and the unseen worlds, between the natural and the supernatural dimensions of time and space, and reveals to us the mysterious domain of angels—mighty, powerful messengers and warriors on assignment from God sent into this dimension to serve Him and us! You will be encouraged as you read this book and discover the role of angels and how they influence the outcomes of your life.

—David Cerullo
Chairman and CEO, Inspiration Ministries

Life can sometimes be complex and overwhelming, especially these days. Our minds and our resources have been stretched to the limit. Just when daily anxiety overwhelms and seems to become the new normal for our lives, Ron Phillips delivers fresh faith and renewed hope with *Our Invisible Allies*.

I have always loved stories of the U.S. military coming to rescue an outnumbered platoon as the enemy closes in. I love stories of the unexpected blessing that bares proof that somehow God will make a way where there seems to be no way for His children.

However, as I read *Our Invisible Allies*, my eyes were opened to a whole new dimension—the dimension where God dwells. I was blown away by the mystery of angels and how God uses these holy beings to guard us every hour of our daily lives.

I'm not the same person when I finished this book that I was when I first began reading it. The stories and the instruction of this book will bring you open doors, fulfilled dreams, and... miracles.

—Alvin Slaughter
International Speaker and Worship Leader

Our INVISIBLE ALLIES

Our INVISIBLE ALLIES

RON PHILLIPS

Charisma
HOUSE
A STRANG COMPANY

Design Director: Bill Johnson
Cover design by Bill Johnson

Library of Congress Cataloging-in-Publication Data:
Phillips, Ron M.
    Our invisible allies / by Ron Phillips. -- 1st ed.
        p. cm.
    Includes bibliographical references.
    ISBN 978-1-59979-523-2
    1. Angels--Christianity. I. Title.
    BT966.3.P45 2009
    235'.3--dc22

                                                2009022144

First Edition

09 10 11 12 13 — 9 8 7 6 5 4 3 2 1
Printed in the United States of America

It is my joy to dedicate this book to:

Dick and Sandy Broadbent, who love God and whose love has given me fresh hope;

Joe and Diane Guthrie, who labor beside me and walk with the angels in the supernatural;

Dave and Marsha Sturm, who give themselves devotedly to serve the kingdom;

and Perry and Pam Stone, whose friendship strengthens me and whose lives and ministry inspire me.

ACKNOWLEDGMENTS

L ET ME THANK MY DEAR WIFE, PAULETTE, FOR HER LOVE and intercession; also for her research.

Let me thank Carolyn Sutton (retired), who typed and preserved the old original studies.

Let me thank the media staff, Angie McGregor and Julie Harding, who helped research and edit the book. (Also thank you for finding the audio version in our archives.)

I send a big thank-you to Trey Gardenhire for his initial input and encouragement as we began this entire project together.

I want to thank Marsha Sturm, who typed each draft with expertise and care.

I am grateful to all the members of Abba's House and all the partners of Ron Phillips Ministry for their unfailing support.

A very special thank-you to the wonderful people at Strang Communications; especially Barbara Dycus for her encouragement from the very beginning and Jevon Bolden for sharing her talents and gifts in editing this project and seeing the work to completion.

CONTENTS

Introduction 1

SECTION ONE
WHERE ANGELS ORIGINATED

Chapter One: The Presence of Angels 7
Chapter Two: The Reality of Angels. 13
Chapter Three: The Mystery of Angels. 21
Chapter Four: The Variety of Angels. 33
Chapter Five: The Appearance of Angels 47
Chapter Six: The Conflict of Angels. 57

SECTION TWO
HOW ANGELS OPERATE

Chapter Seven: Worship—Angels Around the Throne. . .67
Chapter Eight: Destiny—Angels Among the Nations . . 75
Chapter Nine: Protection—Angels on Defense 85
Chapter Ten: Guidance—Angels Out Front 101
Chapter Eleven: Strength—Angels Plugged In 111

SECTION THREE
HOW ANGELS ARE ACTIVATED

Chapter Twelve: Angels Obey Orders. 119
Chapter Thirteen: Angels Respond to Scripture 125
Chapter Fourteen: Angels Answer Prayer 131
Chapter Fifteen: Angels Move on Miracle Ground 141

SECTION FOUR
WHEN ANGELS VINDICATE

Chapter Sixteen: Angels Execute God's Wrath 155

Chapter Seventeen: Angels Escort Believers Home 165

Addendum: Christ Is to Be Worshiped,
                        Not Angels 185

Notes 197

INTRODUCTION

O N DECEMBER 20, 1857, CHARLES SPURGEON DELIV-
ered a sermon called "The First Christmas Carol." In
that sermon Spurgeon spoke of the believer and his
angelic allies. He began his sermon with these words:

Glory to God in the highest, and on earth peace,
good will toward men.

—LUKE 2:14, KJV

It is superstitious to worship angels; it is but proper
to love them. Although it would be a high sin,
and an act of misdemeanor against the Sovereign
Court of Heaven to pay the slightest adoration to
the mightiest angel, yet it would be unkind and
unseemly, if we did not give to holy angels a place
in our heart's warmest love. In fact, he that contem-
plates the character of angels, and marks their many
deeds of sympathy with men, and kindness towards
them, cannot resist the impulse of his nature—the
impulse of love towards them. The one incident in
angelic history, to which our text refers, is enough
to weld our hearts to them forever.

How free from envy the angels were! Christ did
not come from heaven to save their compeers when
they fell. When Satan, the mighty angel, dragged
with him a third part of the stars of heaven, Christ
did not stoop from his throne to die for them; but

he left them to be reserved in chains and darkness until the last great day. Yet angels did not envy men. Though they remembered that he took not up angels, yet they did not murmur when he took up the seed of Abraham; and though the blessed Master had never condescended to take the angel's form, they did not think it beneath them to express their joy when they found him arrayed in the body of an infant.

How free, too, they were from pride! They were not ashamed to come and tell the news to humble shepherds. Methinks they had as much joy in pouring out their songs that night before the shepherds, who were watching with their flocks, as they would have had if they had been commanded by their Master to sing their hymn in the halls of Caesar. Mere men— men possessed with pride, think it a fine thing to preach before kings and princes; and think it great condescension now and then to have to minister to the humble crowd.

Not so the angels. They stretched their willing wings, and gladly sped from their bright seats above, to tell the shepherds on the plain by night, the marvelous story of an Incarnate God. And mark how well they told the story, and surely you will love them! Not with the stammering tongue of him that tells a tale in which he hath no interest; nor even with the feigned interest of a man that would move the passions of others, when he feeleth no emotion himself; but with joy and gladness, such as angels only can know. They *sang* the story out, for they could not stay to tell it in heavy prose. They sang, "Glory to God on high, and on earth peace, good will towards men." Methinks they sang it with gladness in their eyes; with their hearts burning with love, and with breasts as full of joy as if the good news to man had been good news to themselves. And, verily, it was good news to them, for the heart of sympathy makes good news to others, good news to itself.

Do you not love the angels? Ye will not bow before them, and there ye are right; but will ye not love them? Doth it not make one part of your antici- pation of heaven, that in heaven you shall dwell with the holy angels, as well as with the spirits of the just made perfect? Oh, how sweet to think that these holy and lovely beings are our guardians every hour! They keep watch and ward about us, both in the burning noontide, and in the darkness of the night. They keep us in all our ways; they bear us up in their hands, lest at any time we dash our feet against stones. They unceasingly minister unto us who are the heirs of salvation; both by day and night they are our watchers and our guardians, for know ye not, that "the angel of the Lord encampeth round about them that fear him."[1]

As we explore the mystical world of the angels, may we come to love them for their faithful service to the triune God and their tender service to us. May they be welcome in our churches, our homes, and our workplaces. May we enjoy their companionship until they carry us across the great divide to the world where there is no death.

Section One

Where
ANGELS
ORIGINATED

Chapter One

The PRESENCE of ANGELS

But above all else, angels work for the Master of the universe and share in our desire to worship Him and accomplish His will.

D URING OPERATION DESERT STORM IN 1991, THIRTY-five nations formed a coalition with the United States, making a total of thirty-six nations, against Saddam Hussein to bring Kuwait back under the leadership of the emir of Kuwait. This coalition created such a powerful force against Iraq that the air strike began and ended within six weeks. Iraq surrendered after these bombings and a four-day ground campaign.[1]

This operation was extremely successful because the leaders of these countries came together, agreed on a common goal, organized their attack, and created a fair and uniform way to direct their troops, which promoted unity, easy communication, and a shared goal.[2]

Each of these thirty-six countries supplied troops based on their military resources. While the United States and Great Britain supplied the most, every country supplied a particular number of troops to champion the cause. As a result, each nation only had to supply a small amount of resources in order to accomplish the goal of liberating Kuwait from Iraq. The strategy was masterfully executed, and because of the formation of this coalition, the sacrifice from each country was minimal.

Fast-forward to modern America: Did you know the present war in Iraq is the longest war in American history? One of the many reasons for its length and complexity is the absence of allies! Unlike Desert Storm, our nation has had great difficulty finding the needed support for our war, and so, alone and exhausted, this conflict has stretched years beyond what was expected. Unfortunately, this scenario epitomizes the unhappy state of believers living in spiritual defeat! Believers are failing to employ and deploy the hosts of heaven surrounding them. All of the great men and women of faith noted in Holy Scriptures operated with the supernatural assistance of various angels.

If you haven't noticed, there is a growing fascination with angels in our society. For some reason, the possibility of supernatural encounters with angelic beings fascinates this generation. I find this astonishing because as a child of the 1960s, I was reared in an environment dominated by the denial of God and the supernatural, but today, the majority of people believe in unseen spiritual forces that can be channeled and interacted with daily.

When did this drastic shift take place, and why has it happened? As Christians, we should be keenly aware of what others are saying related to unseen forces and remember that angels assist us in ways completely unknown to us.

In their younger days, Coach Mike Dubose and his wife, Polly, had just moved from Chattanooga to Hattiesburg, Mississippi. Polly took a break from unpacking the moving boxes in their new tri-level home to put their precious two-year-old son to bed. Secure in the fact that her son was safe in bed, as he had never climbed out of the baby bed before, Polly went downstairs to continue the task at hand. Unknown to Polly, her sweet baby had climbed out of his crib, slipped outside, found his Big Wheel scooter, and disappeared. As Polly continued to get her house in order, she was totally unaware her son was in harm's way.

There is a growing fascination with angels in our society. The possibility of supernatural encounters with angelic beings fascinates this generation.

As she continued unpacking box after box in the lower level of her beautiful new home, Polly heard a knock at the door. When Polly opened the door, there stood a lady with her son. The woman explained she had found the boy at a busy intersection two blocks away. Now understand that Polly knew no one in Hattiesburg and had just moved to this address. Frightened and startled, Polly turned to set the boy down, then turned back to thank the lady, and there was no one at the door. The lady had just vanished.

Polly never saw or heard from that woman again. Coach and Polly Dubose believe an angel had rescued their son!

Angels are indeed our "allies." Allies are close friends who are willing to:

- Love and protect what you love
- Face a common enemy with you
- Share with you the same allegiances and loyalties
- Obey the same orders
- Make the same sacrifices
- Share similar weapons
- Operate covertly in the enemy's territory when necessary
- Keep open lines of communication
- Stay until the finish
- Operate in ranks under authority
- Move based on written agreement

Angels are friends that help guide, protect, and minister to us so that we may endure in the cause of Christ for our lives.

Think about your own life. When living becomes difficult and you are in short supply of moral support and guidance, the instructions are simple and universal: join hands with your friends, family, spouse, and co-workers. These people are your allies. But be honest; isn't this hard to *do* sometimes? How can allies be trusted in a world full of corruption and decay? Remember the new feeling you discovered when a good friend betrayed you or when a group project fell apart because there was no cooperative effort? What about the loneliness you felt when your own family abandoned you or a loved one cheated on you with someone else? These encounters initiate all of us into the harsh realities of human nature.

Now, let's reevaluate. Isn't the idea of trusting in allies *hard* to believe? Come on, how are we supposed to trust these angelic beings in our spiritual lives? Aren't there some angels who have "fallen"? My purpose in writing this book is for us to discover that the angelic allies around us *are* trustworthy. They will not abandon us in our efforts to spread the gospel to a lost and dying world. My hope and prayer is that you realize angels are friends that help guide, protect, and minister to us so that we may endure in the cause of Christ for our lives.

The will of God consumes and possesses angels, and they passionately pursue His salvation for us. They minister to us in ways that are wholly unique from any guidance we can receive on Earth. They comfort us, speak to us, monitor the spiritual climate around us, teach us, and help us. But above all else, angels work for the Master of the universe and share in our desire to worship Him and accomplish His will. They are our allies.

Chapter Two

The REALITY of ANGELS

"An angel drew me out of the deep waters and took me to heaven, and I saw Uncle Mark and Jesus. Later the angel brought me back."

IT WAS A COLD EVENING IN GADSDEN, ALABAMA, AND despite the wintry weather forecast, I was excited to be traveling into the mountains to preach at a gathering of churches in North Alabama. The late Dr. Claude Rhea, who had sung for Billy Graham, was the featured musical guest, and I at twenty-nine years of age would follow with the message. What a fantastic opportunity for a young preacher! My wife, Paulette, wasn't quite as enthusiastic. She gave me an apprehensive look as I kissed her good-bye. "Be careful, honey. It is snowing," she warned. Not known for my driving skills, I was oblivious to her warning.

As I traveled the sixty miles north into the hills, I noticed the snow beginning to stick to the grass and fields. As I neared the church, snow had already begun to cover the road. However, to my delight, the church was full and the crowd was excited. Dr. Rhea gave a powerful testimony of his healing from cancer and delivered a stirring rendition of the popular Gaither classic "He Touched Me" as the finale to his portion of the evening. The mountain people loved it!

The atmosphere was electric when I stepped up to preach. However, the Spirit wasn't the only thing falling that night; a blanket of snow was covering the region. And because of the weather, the host pastor had asked me to be brief. As I closed the message, the congregation left quickly. I thanked Dr. Rhea for his music and bid a quick farewell to the host pastor, who was getting into his pickup truck and heading home. One man from the church asked if I needed any help getting off the mountain. With little experience driving in ice and snow, I boastfully replied, "I can handle it." As I made my way down the narrow road, my confidence soon disappeared. Snow covered everything, and visibility was difficult due to the falling snow.

The car began to skid, and I braked, sending the car into two 360s, and came to a stop perched on the edge of a steep embankment. Finally, after some time, I got the car turned in the right direction, but I realized I was in trouble. At that moment, I began to pray and ask God for help. I heard His voice speak to my spirit, "Your angel is sitting beside you." At this point in my life, I had not received the baptism of the Spirit, so the supernatural world was strange to me. I looked toward the passenger seat, and to my surprise, there was a faint glow. At first I thought it was simply a reflection from the snow, but then my spirit suddenly became alert and I realized my angel was with me.

The Lord spoke to me and said, "Command your angel to help you." I was ignorant at that juncture of scriptural instruction on the ministry of angels: "Are they not all ministering spirits sent forth to minister for those who will inherit salvation?" (Hebrews 1:14). I spoke to the angel and very timidly said, "Angel, would you go outside and help me not to skid and get safely home?" There was no audible response from the angel, but I knew I was safe to proceed. So I put the car in drive, and the tires gripped the road. With the faint glow now above the right fender, I came off that mountain without another slip or slide of any kind. When I came to Interstate 59, the road I was descending was closed. The state trooper who had closed that mountain road asked me how I had made it. I mumbled, "The Lord helped me..." As I began to close the window he said, "You all be careful." I looked to my right, and for an instant I saw the figure of a person sitting in the seat beside me; the trooper had seen him also. I made it safely home to my wife, who had been praying for me.

I began to pray and ask God for help.
I heard His voice speak to my spirit,
"Your angel is sitting beside you."

What happened on that mountain? I believe one of God's angels came out of the eternal dimension into earthly time to rescue a frightened young preacher. This was not the first time, nor would it be the last time I would experience such a presence. I recalled the two times I was protected while traveling to and from Clarke College in Newton, Mississippi. I left Mont-gomery, Alabama, on Sunday afternoon and headed back across Highway 80 through Selma, Alabama, and Meridian, Mississippi, to Newton, Mississippi. Between Selma and Uniontown, on that two-lane highway, I was forced off the road by an eastbound car that came over the line into my lane. I swerved onto the shoulder and went barreling toward a concrete bridge abutment at sixty-five miles an hour. With little time to react, I braced myself for the impact. A few seconds later, I found myself back on the highway, traveling west perfectly safe. I know there was no physical way I could have missed that bridge. Did an angel move the car?

Later that same year, I was traveling home with a friend in his 1965 Pontiac GTO. He was driving east between Uniontown and Selma when an eighteen-wheeler topped the hill in front of us in our lane as he passed a pickup truck. My friend turned the wheel toward the deep ditch on our right. The tire hit the soft dirt and gravel, and the car flipped over. My friend was ejected from the car and suffered a broken arm, shoulder, and collarbone. As the car rolled over three times, I felt a warm blanket cover me. Something held me safe inside that car even though I was not wearing a seat belt. If I had I fallen out of the car, I would have been crushed. The car stopped upright, and gas was pouring out of the tank, but against all reason I stepped out of the car without a scratch! I looked around for the blanket that had covered me during the accident, but there was none! Who or what covered and protected me? Was it my angel?

Dr. Craig Buettner, a family practitioner from Tuscaloosa, Alabama, and the team physician for the University of Alabama football team, was enjoying a day at the pool with his son's base-ball team. Dr. Buettner and his wife, Amy, led busy lives not only with his medical practice but also with being parents of five children ranging in age from five weeks to nine years old. As everyone settled down to eat with their family and friends, Amy noticed that their four-year-old son, Kennedy, was missing. They began to search the house, the pool, and the neighborhood, but there was no sign of him. Then their nine-year-old son screamed from the pool, dove in, and pulled Kennedy from the pool. Kennedy was bloated, blue, not breathing, and his heart had stopped. Dr. Buettner immediately began CPR on his little boy while Amy began to pray through her sobs. Soon the emergency crew came as Dr. Buettner cleared Kennedy's lungs and triggered a faint heartbeat.

As the car rolled over three times, I felt a warm blanket cover me. Something held me safe inside that car even though I was not wearing a seat belt.

Kennedy was soon transferred from the hospital in Tuscaloosa to the children's hospital in Birmingham, Alabama. The neurologist at the children's hospital only gave a 15 percent chance of survival for little Kennedy with no hope for a "normal" life if he did live. The doctors and nurses worked through the night with Kennedy, and by morning he was much improved. Within eight days, the boy was completely healed and went home with no brain damage at all. When Amy asked Kennedy what happened, the boy said, "An angel drew me out of the deep waters and took me to heaven, and I saw Uncle Mark and Jesus. Later the angel brought me back." Kennedy admitted that he was not afraid.

Interestingly enough, Uncle Mark had died with cancer just six months before Kennedy's accident. Uncle Mark was a deer hunter and was nicknamed "Buckmaster." Of course the angelic intervention aspect of this story is astounding; however, there are two other interesting things you should know. First, the phrase used by Kennedy "drew me out of the deep waters" was part of a scripture given to the Buettners by a close friend.

> He reached down from on high and took hold of me; *he drew me out of deep waters.* He rescued me from my powerful enemy, from my foes, who were too strong for me. They confronted me in the day of my disaster, but the LORD was my support.
> —PSALM 18:16–18, NIV,
> EMPHASIS ADDED

Secondly, the neurologist who helped save the boy's life was working his last day at the children's hospital; his last name was the same as Uncle Mark's nickname. Coincidence? Anomaly? No! Angels visited and saved Kennedy's life.

---

*Angels are a key connection to
the eternal dimension.*

As the years passed I have had countless reports and experiences with our Lord and His holy angels. Angel sightings have occurred in our services at Abba's House. Angelic interventions have been manifested on many occasions. Who are these beings? Where do they live? How do they look? How do they work? What have they done in the past? What are they doing now? What part will they play at the end of the age? How can you activate angelic assistance in your life?

The remaining chapters in this book will open your eyes to another world, the eternal dimension. You will learn that angels are a key connection to that realm for us. It is important for you to know that angelic assistance is not automatic! Angelic operation is consistent with Scripture and the heavenly chain of command. This book will fascinate you, but I hope you will move from fascination to faith, and from faith to facilitation of your heavenly resources.

Chapter Three

The MYSTERY of ANGELS

A miracle is a dimensional interruption when the spiritual world breaks into our mundane existence, changing our limited existence from ordinary to extraordinary. We can live in wonder again!

IMAGINE DAVID SITTING UNDER THE STARS IN THE JUDEAN wilderness after an exhausting day of herding his sheep; the splendor of the sky overwhelms him. In that moment he sees the utter insignificance of man contrasted with the mystery of God. His heart explodes in wonder and praise that God would take time to give thought to man! Beyond that David sees a God who is coming for man.

Here humanity rises to heights of glory! Our God takes notice of us, cares for us, and crowns us as royalty on Earth. However, in this psalm, David reveals to us that our universe, as vast as it is, is not the only realm where life abounds.

> O LORD, our Lord, how excellent is Your name in
> all the earth, who set Your glory above the heavens!
> —PSALM 8:1

Life exists in other dimensions beyond the earth! In fact, supernatural beings exist beyond our earthly realm. Speaking of humanity, the Bible says, "For You have made him a little lower than the angels" (Psalm 8:5). David looked heavenward and saw the majesty of God in the vastness of the created order! He looked to the earth and saw tiny man as the centerpiece and crowning glory of that order! You can hear the music of the supernatural and its rhythm soaring from his ravished soul!

There are other beings from another dimension that are moving by the multitudes across the vast expanse of our known world. These beings are not subject to the limitations of our world. Beyond our normal range of understanding is another dimension more real and lasting than anything we can imagine. The existence of another realm called "the heavenlies" where marvelous creatures both magnificent and malevolent operate is not science fiction. In this realm exist these living beings called angels, along with their dark cousins, demons. Created by God, these timeless beings have a history of their own. Remarkably, they have the ability to come and go between the eternal dimension and our world.

There are realms of reality and life beyond human reach and reason without supernatural assistance. The angels, God's hosts, are among such mysteries. Yes, these supernatural beings are found throughout the Scriptures, from the first page to the last page of the Bible.

Throughout my life, I have been the recipient of angelic assistance. Only recently has science caught up with the Bible in the area of other realms and dimensions beyond normal human perception. Living with us and beyond us at the same time are the angels of God.

Beyond our normal range of understanding is another dimension more real and lasting than anything we can imagine.

THE MYSTERIOUS REALMS OF ANGELS

How old are angels? How old is creation? There is much debate among Christians about the age of the earth. To me it is irrelevant because God lives beyond the limits of the four dimensions of our existence. Time is a product of our universe and its movements, and God lives beyond these limits of human history and its time-driven record.

ANGELS ARE CREATED BEINGS

The hosts of heaven were brought to life by the Creator God. They were given a deathless, timeless existence very different from the history of humans.

> You alone are the LORD; You have made heaven,
> the heaven of heavens, with all their host, the
> earth and everything on it, the seas and all that
> is in them, and You preserve them all. The host of
> heaven worships You.
>
> —NEHEMIAH 9:6

Yahweh, the Lord, created all the "hosts" of heaven, and these "hosts" worship Him. Angels came to life at the command of God. They were commanded and they were created. (See Psalm 148:5.) These wonderful creatures are numberless; though our universe seems empty of life, the heavenly realm teems with energy and life.

This scripture indicates that the angels are created beings and that one of their functions is to praise and worship the Lord. Paul again affirms the fact that angels are created beings. These living beings precede Earth and humanity in the creation.

> For by Him all things were created that are in heaven
> and that are on earth, visible and invisible, whether
> thrones or dominions or principalities or powers. All
> things were created through Him and for Him.
>
> —COLOSSIANS 1:16

Angels were created by the Lord Jesus and for the Lord Jesus. Angels were agents of the creation of our universe.

> Where were you when I laid the foundations of the
> earth? Tell Me, if you have understanding. Who
> determined its measurements? Surely you know! Or
> who stretched the line upon it? To what were its
> foundations fastened? Or who laid its cornerstone,

when the morning stars sang together, and all the
sons of God shouted for joy?

—Job 38:4–7

Job may very well be the oldest book in the Bible. It is full
of mystery and wonder. According to the above scripture, at the
dawn of creation angels were active. When I read these words,
my soul trembles within me; we read and are carried back to the
earliest moments of history.

> *If the visible world is all there is*
> *and life an accident, then human*
> *intelligence, achievements, and*
> *aspirations mean nothing.*

Creation was initiated by a sound... "God said!" His mighty
word sounded forth in what science calls a "big bang." God
spoke, and the great starry host exploded in a fireworks display,
the remnant of which still lights up the sky over our heads. Our
sun still warms us all these ages later from that beginning blast.
Watching this entire demonstration, like a family at a fireworks
display, were the "sons of God," the holy angels. All of these
beings shouted while Creation was being strung into place by
God's hand. The stars were their orchestra as they shouted
with joy!

Earth is a small planet in an average-sized solar system on the
edge of a galaxy called the Milky Way. The vast expanse of the
universe dwarfs our planet. In comparison, the earth would be less

than a grain of sand in a large building! That perspective diminishes the significance of those of us who live on this planet.

If the visible world is all there is and life an accident, then human intelligence, achievements, and aspirations mean nothing. Solomon felt this way after exploring human existence in the present dimension and declared it to be grasping for the wind. Take a look at his words: "And I set my heart to know wisdom and to know madness and folly. I perceived that this also is grasping for the wind" (Ecclesiastes 1:17).

Solomon understood that God has set a desire in humanity for more than what we can see in this life. His quest led him to discover the eternal dimension, a reality beyond the four dimensions of our existence. From Ecclesiastes 3:11 we see this perspective on the eternal world: "He has made everything beautiful in its time. Also He has put eternity in their hearts, except that no one can find out the work that God does from beginning to end."

We live in another dimension; however, we can escape the evil matrix and live in the heavenly dimension where angels operate and miracles happen.

He understood that God has made everything beautiful in its time. It is God who put eternity in our hearts, and the work that God does from beginning to end is on His time schedule. We should rejoice and do well in our lives, and eat and drink and enjoy the good of our labor here on Earth because it is the gift of God. Whatever God does is forever; nothing can be added to it and nothing taken from it. God does it; we should reverence and honor Him. God sees it all—past, present, and future—and we are responsible for what God has entrusted to us. Our lives are connected to an eternal world more real and lasting than the present world.

The most intriguing science fiction films of the past decade were The Matrix trilogy. These movies were fascinating as the characters were living in an artificial world they thought was real. These three movies chronicle the characters' discovery that they are really asleep to the real world, are being manipulated by evil forces, and are prisoners of this dark world. These characters who discover the unseen real world are ridiculed and mocked. Finally, in a powerful scene, the main character dies to reveal the open door to the real world.

This scenario is true of our world. It is temporary! We live in another dimension; however, we can escape the evil matrix and live in the heavenly dimension where angels operate and miracles happen. Paul made the same discovery regarding the heavenly realm and declared this fascinating truth:

> Therefore we do not lose heart. Even though our outward man is perishing, yet the inward man is being renewed day by day. For our light affliction, which is but for a moment, is working for us a far more exceeding and eternal weight of glory, while we do not look at the things which are seen, but at the things which are not seen. For the things which are seen are temporary, but the things which are not seen are eternal.
>
> —2 Corinthians 4:16–18

There is an unseen world that is greater, more real, and more lasting than our limited existence.

UNSEEN WORLD

Quantum physics studies the origin of matter. This realm of science believes the world had a beginning; therefore, a greater world existed and still thrives beyond our cosmos. On earth, we live in four dimensions; we live in a world with length, width, height, and time. In the natural, these dimensions limit us. Quantum physicists like Brian Greene, who wrote *The Elegant Universe*, have discovered the existence of at least eleven dimensions. All of these dimensions are moving in straight lines. This perspective of history is called "linear." God created our universe and set this line of history in motion. He created it, but He is not captive to it. God lives above and beyond our history. Knowing that there are at least seven other dimensions beyond our limited view, our perspective is broadened and our imagination captivated by dimensions we have not seen.

This is the realm where God abides! Paul called these dimensions "the third heaven." Solomon, at the dedication of the great temple, spoke of our God not limited to the heavens we observe. "But will God indeed dwell on the earth? Behold, heaven and the heaven of heavens cannot contain You. How much less this temple which I have built!" (1 Kings 8:27).

How do we reach the dimension where God dwells? Our linear history cannot reach the third heaven; these dimensions do not move in the same direction. However, His dimensions may intersect with ours. When that happens, all that is in the new (or God) dimension, according to quantum physics, becomes available in our present dimension. When these dimensions intersect, the limitations and laws of our present dimension can be altered, broken, or transformed. The limits and laws of our four-dimensional world can be suspended. Our natural order can be changed by a supernatural dimensional interruption!

A miracle is a dimensional interruption when the spiritual world breaks into our mundane existence,[1] changing our limited existence from ordinary to extraordinary. We can live in wonder again! The impossible becomes possible, and hope flourishes.

Though the planet Earth is but a speck of dust in the vast ocean of the universe, the Hubble telescope proves that the four-dimensional arena in which humanity lives strains human reason in terms of size. The mega-size of creation is outdone by its awesome beauty.

A miracle is a dimensional interruption when the spiritual world breaks into our mundane existence, changing our limited existence from ordinary to extraordinary.

When we put down the telescope and look into a microscope, we discover that one cell of the human body contains vast amounts of information. One set of twenty-four human chromosomes contains 3.1 billion patterns of DNA code.[2] It is absolutely incredible!

> I will praise You, for I am fearfully and wonderfully made; marvelous are Your works, and that my soul knows very well. My frame was not hidden from You, when I was made in secret, and skillfully wrought in the lowest parts of the earth. Your eyes

saw my substance, being yet unformed. And in Your book they all were written, the days fashioned for me, when as yet there were none of them.

—PSALM 139:14–16

Dr. Francis Collins, who sequenced the human genome and unraveled our DNA, is a Christian. He said, "The solution is actually readily at hand, once one ceases to apply human limitations to God. If God is outside of nature, then He is outside of space and time. In that context, God could in the moment of creation of the universe also know every detail of the future. That could include the formation of the stars, planets, and galaxies, all of the chemistry, physics, geology, and biology that led to the formation of life on earth, and the evolution of humans, right to the moment of your reading this book—and beyond."[3]

Long before *Star Wars*, the ancient prophets saw an End Time life-and-death struggle between the forces of darkness and the forces of light in the eternal realm. Though the war has been won by Christ at the cross, a battle rages for the soul of mankind; we are not alone in that battle. We have invisible allies available to assist us in the End Time as we enforce Christ's victory.

UNSEEN BEINGS

Other beings live in the eternal dimension. These are the real ETs (extraterrestrials). Paul called this realm "the heavenlies." This realm is not geographical! This eternal dimension can be as close as one's breath! Angels live in this realm but are allowed to cross over into our four-dimensional world! Our Lord Jesus came out of that realm into this realm to reveal to us the way home! Angels move interdimensionally in order to operate on our behalf. Angels, without number, accompany us now.

A battle rages for the soul of mankind, yet we are not alone in that battle. We have invisible allies available to assist us in the End Time as we enforce Christ's victory.

In this exciting time in history, angelic activity and involvement are on the increase as we move toward the climax of history. Two worlds, the spirit realm and the physical realm, are on a collision course that will culminate in Christ's return.

Chapter Four

The VARIETY *of* ANGELS

Let us get to know these friends and allies so we may enlist their aid in the great mission to which we are called.

THE HOSTS

How does God operate in our world? He moves through people and angels! Earlier I shared that angels are called "hosts." This name has to do with the vast numbers of these spiritual beings available to serve! How many angels are there? No one except God can count them: "The chariots of God are twenty thousand, even thousands of thousands" (Psalm 68:17). "...an innumerable company of angels..." (Hebrews 12:22). "...and the number of them was ten thousand times ten thousand and thousands of thousands..." (Revelation 5:11).

The point is that there are plenty of those wonderful friends available at just the right moment to help us. This was certainly true on the evening of March 6, 1996, as a fierce storm blew into East Tennessee. Dana and Julie Harding had almost completed building their 3,700-square-foot two-story home. The lower level housed Dana's recording studio and business, while their family lived on the second level.

Dana and Julie had done much of the work during the construction of their dream home, along with the help of friends and family. The house was 98 percent complete; all that was needed were gutters, drainage, and some backfill work.

When they went to bed that spring evening, a storm was starting to brew. By 3:45 a.m., it had reached full force. "There was a huge clap of thunder that shook the house and woke me up," recalled Dana, a very sound sleeper who had actually slept through an earthquake once. "Something inside of me told me to go to the basement. I looked out the window, and it looked like a waterfall coming off of the roof—a solid sheet of water."

Dana went down to the then-unfinished recording studio. "We had just moved in four days before, and the studio space was just a big, open room." Except for a couple of support walls and some boxes stacked against the east wall, there was nothing there. Dana walked across to the opposing wall and looked at it. First, shock gripped him, then horror set in as he saw the first signs of impending disaster.

"When I looked at the wall," Dana said, "I saw a crack beginning to form." The crack was about five feet up the ten-foot block wall and was running horizontal the entire length of the fifty-two-foot foundation wall. When the rain came off of the roof, it poured down along the foundation of the new house. Several tons of loose fill dirt unexpectedly settled instantly and created a trap for the water where it could not escape from around the foundation. More water poured off of the roof with no place to go other than to put extreme amounts of pressure on the foundation walls—walls that were never meant to withstand the untold tons of water pressure being exerted on them.

Dana ran up the stairs and woke Julie with the news that the walls were cracking. Julie got out of the bed, put on a robe, sat down on the couch, and began praying. Dana was immediately on the phone with Mike, his good friend and builder, who assured him that he was on the way. Within ten minutes, Mike was there, assessing the situation.

> *"I saw the downstairs, and there were angels standing around the perimeter, lining the walls of the basement."*

"This is really bad. I'm going to get my work van [with all of the tools], and I will be right back," Mike declared.

The crack in the wall had opened up to about a half-inch and showed no signs of stopping. To make matters infinitely worse, the thirty-two-foot end wall was beginning to show signs of stress and was beginning to crack as well. As Mike flew down the dark, wet streets, formulating a plan of action in a mind that just went from peaceful sleep to waking nightmare, Dana went out into the maelstrom to attempt to divert the potential disaster that was coming, fighting the rain, mud, wind, cold, and the desire to fall facedown in the mud and scream.

But all the while, Julie prayed.

And God showed up.

Actually, to be more precise, He sent His angelic messengers. As Julie sat inside praying, wide-awake at this point, she suddenly had a vision. "I saw the downstairs, and there were angels standing around the perimeter, lining the walls of the basement." She initially thought that they were there to support the walls so they would not cave in. As their true purpose was revealed, the reality of the situation became even more miraculous.

At about 4:30 a.m., forty-five minutes after the whole series of disastrous events began, Mike pulled back into the driveway with his work van. A cold, wet, and muddy Dana met him as they walked into the basement (the house was built into a hill, so one end of the house actually had an outside door, with three sides being predominantly underground). When Mike saw the wall and the crack that had tripled in size since the time he left, he exclaimed, "Get Julie out of the house NOW!"

Dana sprinted up the stairs, picked Julie up, and got her out into Mike's still-running van. Mike escaped right behind them. Then it happened...

Within sixty seconds of getting out of the house, the entire fifty-two-foot span of foundation wall collapsed. A tidal wave of mud, rock, water, and various other objects came flooding into the basement. As Dana stood in the rain and watched his dreams cave in with the wall, he recalls thinking, "God, if the whole thing is coming down, just let me be in there when it does."

Now, normally in such a situation, once one wall caves in, the house above it would, at the very least, sag several inches. This would create a chain-reaction of cracked drywall, broken tile, misaligned doorways, broken glass, and a host of other problems.

However, since the far end wall had extreme amounts of pressure against it, was cracking, and had already lost one side support wall, once the end wall collapsed, the house would basically shift, and the whole thing would cave into the hole that had been the basement. "I was at my wits end. I was just waiting for the other shoe to drop," Dana recalls.

It never did.

Julie later realized that although she thought the angels in her vision were there to keep the walls from collapsing, they were, in fact, holding the house up. God supernaturally showed her the angelic hosts who were there protecting them from what could have been catastrophic loss. The end wall, as damaged as it was and with as much pressure as it was bearing, never let go. The side of the house that was suddenly left with no support under it sagged less than three-eighths of an inch. There was virtually no damage to the inside of the house. "Unless you knew exactly where to look," Dana stated, "there was no damage. In fact, all of the damage that was done was hairline fractures in drywall joints and a couple of bathroom tiles that have almost unnoticeable fractures in them. Basically, the kind of stuff that would have happened over time as the house settled anyway."

> *The English word* angel *comes from the Greek word* aggelos, *found in the original New Testament. This word means "a herald or a messenger."*

Over the next several hours, as the cavalry of friends and workers arrived to help, the house was shored up, and the situation was downgraded from "life-threateningly dangerous" to "how many wheelbarrows full of mud can you remove from a basement?" Through the whole experience, and to this day, Dana is still amazed: "Through the whole day and through all of the chaos, Julie was the rock. I was exhausted and ready to throw in the towel, but God had given Julie the vision and had allowed her to see that the angels were there protecting us and supporting us. There was peace in her that, at the time, I didn't understand. I could only see in the natural the chain of events that happened and what the logical conclusion *should* have been. God showed Julie what the true reality of the situation was."

Just as Jacob had a dream of angels, so did Julie at Sea Level Studios, and their home still stands. By the way, my daily radio program is recorded in that miracle place! The hosts are available to us all.

ANGELS

The "hosts" are also called "angels." The English word *angel* comes from the Greek word *aggelos*, found in the original New Testament. This word means "a herald or a messenger."

In the Old Testament the word translated "angel" is *malak*, which means "a message sent." This, of course, indicates that God uses angels to communicate. In a later chapter, we will see how we can receive faith and direction from these amazing allies.

Angels are the "unbegotten" sons of God, while Jesus is the "only" begotten Son of God.

Allies are supernatural creatures of high intelligence. They are a part of our kingdom family. In Hebrews 12:22 we read of an "innumerable company of angels" gathered with the church at worship. Obviously the angels are God's "communication specialists" to Earth.

All of us are aware of the financial meltdown in late 2008. Two weeks before the crisis broke, I was praying in my basement study when I felt a breeze and a presence in the room. As I prayed, I heard in my spirit a voice saying, "Make your retirement safe!" Instead of obeying the angelic visitor, I called my representative at our Christian retirement agency, and he advised against moving the money. Consequently I experienced loss, as did most of the country. I am firmly convinced that God sent an angel to advise me, and I did not listen.

SONS OF GOD

Angels are also called "sons of God." This title is primarily used in the Old Testament, and it speaks of their relationship with God the Father. "Again there was a day when the sons of God came to present themselves before the LORD" (Job 2:1).

Angels are the "unbegotten" sons of God, while Jesus is the "only" begotten Son of God (John 3:16). Those of us who are Christians are now also "sons of God." "Beloved, now we are the sons of God" (1 John 3:1). God is Father to us all, and we are part of an eternal cosmic family.

CHERUBIM

Some angels are called cherubim; they guard the throne of God upon the earth. It appears, from what we read in Scripture, they accompany God when He manifests Himself on Earth. "And He rode upon a cherub, and flew; He flew upon the wings of the wind" (Psalm 18:10).

Cherubim are first mentioned in Genesis 3:24 when they are placed east of Eden to guard the way to the tree of life. This is very interesting because the word *cherubim* comes from an ancient word that means "great, mighty, and gracious to bless!"[1] These are clearly the attributes of God! There at Eden it would seem that these cherubim are hostile to humans in that they guard the way to the tree of life.

On the contrary; they are exhibiting grace, for if Adam ate of that tree, he would be cursed to live in an aging body forever! It was grace that set the cherubim there for us.

I believe Adam and his family brought their offering to the gates of Eden where these cherubim were stationed. Here, a blood sacrifice was offered by our ancient family. It is interesting to see later in Scripture that cherubim of beautiful gold adorned the holy of holies around the bloody mercy seat in the tabernacle and temple. They also adorned the ark of the covenant. These beautiful creatures were a reminder of all that was lost beyond the garden gate and man's need for a Savior.

The real cherubim abode in the tabernacle when the cloud of glory, called the Shechinah, appeared above the mercy seat. Angels guarded the presence of God. When God was not honored, angels were activated to defend God's throne.

> And there I will meet with you, and I will speak with you from above the mercy seat, from between the two cherubim which are on the ark of the Testimony, about everything which I will give you in commandment to the children of Israel.
>
> —EXODUS 25:22

These cherubim later appear in the Book of Ezekiel, chapter 10, where they are described as having four faces, wings, and wheels as a means of conveyance. This would seem to go along with the idea of God's chariot drivers transporting God's throne on the earth!

Later these same beings are observed in Revelation 4 and are called "living ones," in English, and in Greek, *zoon*, from which we get our English word *zoo*. Cherubim are angelic forces related to the planet Earth and its creative order. The four faces exhibit this truth as the number four traditionally represents the earth in early times.

When God was not honored, angels
were activated to defend God's throne.

In the next chapter, I will discuss Lucifer, who was the chief cherub, how he became Satan, and how that affects Earth.

SERAPHIM

Some of the heavenly beings are called seraphim. This is only found in Isaiah 6 when the great prophet had his transforming vision. Isaiah's king and cousin, Uzziah, had died, and the prophet went into the forbidden holy of holies! In his grief, he needed a word from God even if he died in His presence. Upon entering the holy of holies, Isaiah saw the Lord high and lifted up in majesty and glory! In this place, seraphim worshiped God crying, "Holy, holy, holy." As Isaiah looked upon this scene, he was provoked to confess his own unworthiness. A seraph brought a coal of fire from the altar where the blood sacrifice burned and placed it upon the prophet's lips, cleansing him and redirecting his life.

Seraphim means "burning ones"; it would appear there is a direct link between these angels and the manifest presence of God. These are the beings that set our hearts on fire for God's holiness, His presence, and His power! (See Isaiah 6:1–7.)

MICHAEL

Michael, whose name means "who is like God," is mentioned in both the Old and New Testaments, where we discover he is the commander and chief of the angelic armies related to Earth. In the Book of Daniel, it is Michael who came to the aid of the angel who was warring against the demonic prince of Persia for two weeks in order to answer Daniel's prayers. (See Daniel 10:13.) Michael is also found in Revelation 12:7 at the end of the age as the one who casts Satan and the fallen angels out of the heavenlies. In today's vernacular, Michael would be known as the secretary of war!

The angel of the Lord has mighty power. He knows and operates for the people who dwell in the presence of God.

GABRIEL

This mighty angel shows up to answer prayer, interpret dreams, and release the word of God. If Michael is secretary of war, then Gabriel is vice president of communications. He interpreted dreams for Daniel on two separate occasions. Gabriel also brought the word to Mary that even though she was a virgin, she would bear a child, Jesus, the Son of God. Gabriel said of himself that he "stands in the presence of God" (Luke 1:19). This indicates that, along with Michael, Gabriel is the highest rank of angelic authority.

Could this angel have a special assignment to watch over salvation? In Isaiah 63:9 we read, "In all their affliction He was afflicted, and the Angel of His Presence saved them." Some believe the angel of His presence is the preincarnate Christ; clearly this angel is not but is Gabriel.

ANGEL OF THE LORD

The term "angel of the Lord" is mentioned sixty-three times in Scripture. Like the angel of His presence, many believe this angel is the preincarnate Christ. This is impossible as this angel appears twelve times in the New Testament. This angel and the angel of His presence could possibly be the same being. This angel carries an awesome anointing, so much so that God's presence is recognized then worshiped whenever this angel appears. This leads me to believe this angel is God's accompanying angel.

The angel of the Lord has mighty power. He knows and operates for the people who dwell in the presence of God. It was this angel that stayed the hand of Abraham from killing Isaac...that stretched his sword over Jerusalem, causing its destruction in David's day...that killed 185,000 of the Assyrian army in one night...that ordered the watching angels to do surveillance of the whole earth in Zechariah. Also we see the angel of the Lord directed the heavenly choir over the shepherds' field in Bethlehem, appeared to Joseph and Mary to guide them to safety in Egypt, and struck Peter to awaken him and lead him out of prison.

PRINCIPALITIES, POWERS, THRONES, AND DOMINIONS

These are titles of angels who rank over regions, nations, cities, and communities. These can be either good or evil beings. There is a struggle in the invisible realm, known as the heavenlies, between angels of light and those of darkness. This struggle is affected by our prayers. In a later chapter we will say more about the fallen angels. Angels are organized into ranks and operate in a military fashion. Also, all angels have names, distinct personalities, and specific assignments.

As the church comes to the end of herself and realizes the impossibility of her task, the threat of demonic terror, and the rising opposition of a secular society, she will engage the supernatural resources available from God. The church will discover an open heaven, and the hosts, the angelic armies, will come to our aid!

Angels are organized into ranks and operate in a military fashion.

Billy Graham has said, "Angels belong to a uniquely different dimension of creation that we, limited to the natural order, can scarcely comprehend. In this angelic domain the limitations are different from those God has imposed on our natural order. He has given angels higher knowledge, power, and mobility than we; they are God's messengers whose chief business is to carry out His orders in the world. He has given them an ambassadorial charge. He has designated and empowered them as holy deputies to perform works of righteousness. In this way they assist Him as their creator while His sovereignty controls the universe. So He has given them the capacity to bring His holy enterprises to a successful conclusion."[2]

Let us get to know these friends and allies so we may enlist their aid in the great mission to which we are called. Angels are waiting for our call.

Chapter Five

The
APPEARANCE *of*
ANGELS

"I had seen an angel. I couldn't tell you what he looked like, but I saw him. Like the wind when it unfurls a flag, I saw the angel by the force of his action."

I N 1994 OUR CHURCH BEGAN EXPERIENCING AN OUTBREAK of angelic sightings. This continues today. Angels walked into a youth gathering one Wednesday night. They were described as ten- to twelve-foot-tall beings glowing in amber and white.

In our previous sanctuary, on two occasions angels exploded balls of fire in the sanctuary that were both visible and loud. On one of these occasions, it was directly over my head, occurring as I rebuked demonic forces. On the other occasion, a layman, whose teenagers were on drugs, took authority over the enemy in our pulpit, and again angelic fire was manifested. This happened in Scripture to Manoah in the Book of Judges, chapter 13, as the angel of the Lord ascended in the fire!

> *Fear swept over me, but I was not unprepared for this moment. God had me on a journey, and it was time for an object lesson.*

Later, there appeared two angels on the platform who have now moved into our new sanctuary with us. Both stand slightly behind me and to my right hand. One is a towering figure who stands almost the height of the building; the other is smaller and stands nearer and is known as our "joy angel." On many occasions, those who also stand to my right may find themselves tickled or laughing for no apparent reason; this has happened to me dozens of times. Although these angels are not visible to everyone, those who see in the spiritual realm have observed them. Even those who cannot see them have experienced their ministry. Jennie Griesemer had such an experience; I will let her tell you in her own words.

> Although more than fifteen years have passed, the memory is still strong and clear in my mind of the day I "saw" an angel. Morgan and Kayla were both just toddlers, buckled securely in their car seats behind me. It was our errand day, and I was diligently completing my tasks. Our next stop was to deliver some products from my small direct sales business to a new customer who lived in Grant

Estates off Dietz Road in Ringgold, Georgia, where we lived at the time. She had instructed me to leave the products on her front porch and for no reason was I to go into the fenced backyard. "We have a Chow dog back there who is very vicious. He has even bitten family members," she warned, "so just leave the order by the front door. It will be fine."

I drove into the subdivision and up a steep ridge to a secluded cul-de-sac where my customer's home stood alone surrounded by woods. After parking in the driveway, I grabbed the box of products, headed up the sidewalk, up the front stairs, and onto the front porch where I deposited my load by the front door. Turning to leave, I froze in panic at the top of the stairs, for at the bottom of the steps stood that Chow dog, teeth bared, growling viciously, and poised to attack. Fear swept over me, but I was not unprepared for this moment. God had me on a journey, and it was time for an object lesson.

"No temptation has overtaken you except such as is common to man; but God is faithful, who will not allow you to be tempted beyond what you are able, but with the temptation will also make the way of escape, that you may be able to bear it" (1 Corinthians 10:13).

Through the Bible teaching of a man named Kenneth Copeland, God had been instructing me in the nature of fear and faith. I had come to understand that fear is the same spiritual force as faith, but moving in reverse gear. Whereas faith is produced by hearing the Word of God, fear comes by hearing and believing wrong things. Fear is a twisted form of faith; it is faith in the enemy's ability to harm. No wonder Jesus instructed repeatedly, "Fear not." Fear and faith are mutually exclusive and, like forward and reverse gear, cannot operate in the same heart at the same time.

Faith is produced by hearing the Word of God; fear comes by hearing and believing wrong things. Fear is a twisted form of faith; it is faith in the enemy's ability to harm.

Like a big red flag, the awareness of fear reminded me that I must not yield to it. By the grace of God, I declared aloud, "I WILL NOT FEAR!" As quickly as the force had swept over me, it retreated. With a clear mind now, I responded with faith in the Word of God in my heart (Psalms 91:9–11; 103:20; Hebrews 1:14). I spoke aloud what God in His mercy had abundantly stored up in my heart over the preceding weeks and months of training: "Angels, I charge you in the name of Jesus to move this dog down the sidewalk, put him back in his fence, and let me pass safely back to my car."

Suddenly, the fierce eyes of that animal, which until that moment had been intensely fixed on me, popped open. I saw a stunned look in his eyes. Then his head was pressed down to the sidewalk as if an invisible hand had taken hold of his neck. He responded with a growl of futile resistance as the invisible hand turned him 90 degrees to face down the sidewalk. As the invisible hand dragged him, the dog growled and pulled against the force that moved him away from me. I followed behind the animal, pointing the way, thanking God for His angel of protection. "Thank You, God, for Your angels. Thank You for hearkening to my voice. Keep going, now. Put him in that back fence..."

At the end of the sidewalk, the captive dog turned left toward the back gate, and I turned right to get into my car. Safely inside the car, the adrenaline that had pumped through me left me a bit weak, and I began to tremble. I had seen an angel. I couldn't tell you what he looked like, but I saw him. Like the wind when it unfurls a flag, I saw the angel by the force of his action on that dog. Indeed, angels are "ministering spirits sent forth to minister for those who will inherit salvation" (Hebrews 1:14).

As we look through Scripture and history, angels appeared many different ways. Angels are not all alike in their appearance and function. In Scripture, angels often took on the appearance of men. Some angels have wings; others do not. Angels seem to be able to assume whatever shape is necessary to perform their function. Angels often act as we do—eating and drinking, talking and singing. Yet they appear as wind or fire; they also appear as spirits.

Angels are spirit beings.

Angels seem to have a spiritual body suited for the heavenly dimension. A spiritual body is not subject to the limitations of our earth suits or bodies. First Corinthians 15:44 says, "It is sown a natural body, it is raised a spiritual body. There is a natural body, and there is a spiritual body."

Our bodies as they are cannot access the spiritual dimensions. Angels and demons can pass through what we call solid objects and are not limited to our space and time.

It would appear the angels operate in a spiritual body not subject to the laws of nature in our four-dimensional realm. Our bodies in the afterlife will be like the angels: "For in the resurrection they neither marry nor are given in marriage, but are like angels of God in heaven" (Matthew 22:30).

Angels are soldiers.

As we have observed, angels are called "hosts" more than any other title given to them. The word for "hosts" is translated by some as "angel armies." Angels have access to weapons in the spiritual realm. As we have already observed, angels are mighty soldiers in the heavenly realm. Recall in Daniel chapter 10 that Daniel saw and heard the words of the angel after three weeks of fasting and prayer. The appearance of the angel was "clothed in linen, whose waist was girded with gold.... His body was like beryl, his face like the appearance of lightning, his eyes like torches of fire, his arms and feet like burnished bronze in color, and the sound of his words like the voice of a multitude" (Daniel 10:5–6). Daniel alone saw, described, and heard the declaration of the angel. The angel had been hindered by the prince of Persia. The battle between the two had waxed strong and delayed the angel from coming to Daniel. It was only when Michael the archangel came to assist and fight with the enemy that Daniel could hear the heavenly message.

In this passage the curtain is lifted momentarily to reveal the heavenly battles that angels, demons, and believers are engaged in. Not only did the angel fight in the heavens for Daniel, but he also then comforted, reassured, strengthened, and instructed Daniel on the End Times.

Angels are mighty in battle and take up the cause of believers and of Israel. The battle is the Lord's, and it rages in the invisible realms.

These mighty angels, by their very nature, are miracle-working beings full of God-given power and might.

Angels operate in the supernatural realm.

Paul describes angels as "mighty" in 2 Thessalonians.

> …and to give you who are troubled rest with us when the Lord Jesus is revealed from heaven with His mighty angels.
>
> —2 THESSALONIANS 1:7

When translated from the Greek, this word *mighty* is *dunamis*, which means "innate supernatural power." These mighty angels, by their very nature, are miracle-working beings full of God-given power and might. Angels are agents of miracles and the supernatural power of God even in our day!

Angels are swift in their movements.

On closer observation angels seem to move at the speed of thought; sometimes they move so quickly they simply "appear" on the scene. They are not limited by our time or history as they soar through our atmosphere and the solar system; they are truly the ultimate UFOs.

> Then I saw another angel flying in the midst of heaven, having the everlasting gospel to preach to those who dwell on the earth—to every nation, tribe, tongue, and people.
>
> —REVELATION 14:6

Man envies the angels, for we long to fly! From the Wright brothers' first attempts to the emerging technology that enables us to live in space, man has a compulsion to explore beyond the confines of our four dimensions as the angels do. Neil Armstrong, commander of the Apollo flight that put the first man on the moon, said, "Pilots take no special joy in walking. Pilots like flying."[1] We all, whether given opportunity or limited by life's circumstances, long to soar in that heavenly dimension. One day we will fly with the heavenly hosts.

Angels are strong.

Angels appear as strong, tireless creatures who, as we read in Revelation 4:8, do not rest day or night from their worship. Angels have an anointing of strength that flows in the atmosphere of worship; unlike us, they do not tire in war, worship, or ministry.

Angels are systematic.

Angels do not deviate from order or rank. They operate according to the commands of God, knowing their purpose and ministry as they remain faithful in the execution of these duties. There is no doubt that you may have trafficked with angels. You may not have recognized them, as many times they take on human form and cannot be distinguished from humans, but they were in your company.

Chapter Six

The CONFLICT of ANGELS

The good news for all of us is that there are two angels for every demon. These faithful allies have been battle-tested and proven in the timeless ages of the past.

IN THE MONUMENTAL WORK *EARTH'S EARLIEST AGES*, G. H. Pember declared that there was a primeval earth that experienced colossal catastrophe.[1] Pember convincingly proves that something happened between Genesis 1:1 and Genesis 1:2 that made the earth "without form, and void." In Isaiah 45:12, Isaiah declares that God did not make the earth "without form, and void." What occurred on Earth before the planting of the Garden of Eden? Could there have been a world in which a cherub named

Lucifer ruled and covered the earth from a land called Eden? In the prophetic lamentation to the king of Tyre, God speaks through Ezekiel to describe this ancient world and its anointed leader, the angel Lucifer.

Satan desires the Creator's position, preeminence, people, and power. He wants to sit on "the mount of the congregation." Satan and the fallen angels desire to dominate the worship of the people of God!

Ezekiel 28 takes us back, beyond our history, to a land of Eden prior to the garden. Lucifer is described as "the seal of perfection, full of wisdom and perfect in beauty" (verse 12). Furthermore, we are told, while still perfect, he ruled over a land called Eden. "You were in Eden, the garden of God" (verse 13). In that garden, this angel king was covered in great wealth and also surrounded by a vast amount of musical instruments. In fact, Lucifer was created to be the covering of God's new planet, Earth. "You were the anointed cherub who covers; I established you; you were on the holy mountain of God; you walked back and forth in the midst of fiery stones" (verse 14). Here was a creature created perfect by God to rule over the primeval earth, to lead its creatures in worship, and to release the creative resources of God from the fiery stones to all on Earth. Lucifer was anointed for that high purpose, yet Lucifer committed iniquity even though he was created perfect. "You were perfect in your ways from the day you were created, till iniquity was found in you" (verse 15). This word *iniquity* means "to twist or pervert." Lucifer began to crave the worship for himself! God cast Lucifer out of his leadership role: "Therefore I cast you....out of the mountain of God; and I destroyed you, O covering cherub, from the midst of the fiery stones" (verse 16). God cast Lucifer out because of pride: "Your heart was lifted up" (verse 17).

Isaiah confirmed this prophetic word, giving us another account of this momentous event. "How you are fallen from heaven, O Lucifer, son of the morning!" (Isaiah 14:12).

Lucifer's fall took place in the ancient Eden. When he fell, the old earth was destroyed as if an asteroid had hit! All life was abolished, and the earth became without form and void. In that rebellion one-third of the angelic hosts fell with him.

> And another sign appeared in heaven: behold, a great, fiery red dragon having seven heads and ten horns, and seven diadems on his heads. His tail drew a third of the stars of heaven and threw them to the earth. And the dragon stood before the woman who was ready to give birth, to devour her Child as soon as it was born.
>
> —REVELATION 12:3–4

Notice that these angels fell to the earth; this was a part of that ancient catastrophe. Lucifer became Satan, the archenemy of God and His purpose for man! Satan desires the Creator's position, preeminence, people, and power. He wants to sit on "the mount of the congregation" (Isaiah 14:13). Satan and the fallen angels desire to dominate the worship of the people of God!

God's Plan Is Man

God came again to the ruined planet, made it habitable, and planted a garden in the same place—Eden. He then created man, but lurking in that garden was a serpent possessed by Satan. A new king of the earth had come, and Satan came to usurp man's position. Adam and Eve fell, and consequently, all humanity fell, leaving fallen humanity and hosts of demons to inhabit this earthy dimension.

As the second Adam, Jesus Christ would die and be raised from the dead in order to defeat Satan and the fallen angels and also to redeem fallen humanity. God would create a new humanity in Christ.

Demons live to thwart Christians from fulfilling their purpose. Operating in stealth, they secretly seek to subvert the will of God.

The Characteristics of the Enemy of God's Plan

Though the battle has been won, we still face the dark forces of Satan until the end of the age. Notice the characteristics of these dark forces:

Demonic features

The Bible speaks of these fallen angels as sinners. These created beings were involved in wars and conspiracies against the

Most High: "For if God did not spare the angels who sinned, but cast them down to hell and delivered them into chains of darkness, to be reserved for judgment…" (2 Peter 2:4).

They are all rebels by nature. They are evil and fierce. These unholy angels exhibit wickedness, iniquities, and unlawful deeds under the angel of darkness. Psalm 78:49 says, "He cast on them the fierceness of His anger, wrath, indignation, and trouble, by sending angels of destruction among them."

Demonic function

Demons are organized into ranks called principalities, powers, rulers of darkness, and spiritual forces of wickedness. These powers are associated with demonic possession and witchcraft as they influence human beings. Even in Shakespeare's *Macbeth*, Lady Macbeth invoked the powers of evil, the "murdering ministers" and "sightless substances" that "wait on nature's mischief."[2] Scripture reveals their nature this way.

> For we do not wrestle against flesh and blood, but against principalities, against powers, against the rulers of the darkness of this age, against spiritual hosts of wickedness in the heavenly places.
> —EPHESIANS 6:12

Demons live to thwart Christians from fulfilling their purpose. Operating in stealth, they secretly seek to subvert the will of God. In 1 Timothy 4:1, these evil ones are called deceitful and seducing spirits as well as the spirits of error: "Now the Spirit expressly says that in latter times some will depart from the faith, giving heed to deceiving spirits and doctrines of demons."

"And no wonder! For Satan himself transforms himself into an angel of light" (2 Corinthians 11:14).

They operate in deception particularly where truth is rejected. By doing this, demons work destruction on the earth and cause grave trouble by manipulation.

Demonic forces already bound

Some ranks of fallen angels were so vile God has bound them in chains of darkness.

> Now it came to pass, when men began to multiply on the face of the earth, and daughters were born to them, that the sons of God saw the daughters of men, that they were beautiful; and they took wives for themselves of all whom they chose. And the LORD said, "My Spirit shall not strive with man forever, for he is indeed flesh; yet his days shall be one hundred and twenty years." There were giants on the earth in those days, and also afterward, when the sons of God came in to the daughters of men and they bore children to them. Those were the mighty men who were of old, men of renown.
> —GENESIS 6:1–4

Some demons cohabited with women, and the offspring of the union created giants on the earth. These giants could be the source of the so-called gods of mythology of the ancient world. In the New Testament they are called "the angels who sinned" (2 Peter 2:4).

These angels left their own house, took up residence in human hosts, and bred a hybrid race of wicked, vile humans.

Christ's preaching to them

Peter speaks of Christ preaching to "the spirits in prison." Here Jesus Christ came during the three days He was absent from Earth after His crucifixion and prior to His resurrection.

> By whom also He went and preached to the spirits in prison, who formerly were disobedient, when once the Divine longsuffering waited in the days of Noah, while the ark was being prepared, in which a few, that is, eight souls, were saved through water.
>
> —1 Peter 3:19–20

We know that these certain demons were confined by God. Though the word *preach* is used in the passage, it is not *evangelion*, which means "to preach the gospel," but *kerusso* in Greek, which means "to proclaim or announce." This passage is directed to demons. There is no gospel preached to men after death. "And as it is appointed for men to die once, but after this the judgment" (Hebrews 9:27).

Furthermore, there is no special prison for humans who sinned in Noah's day. Jesus Christ died and descended into Hades. He dropped off the dying thief in paradise and went to the place of torments. He announced His victory to these confined demons: "...who has gone into heaven and is at the right hand of God, angels and authorities and powers having been made subject to Him" (1 Peter 3:22).

In the realm of eternity, the enemy's most powerful demons were totally humiliated: "Having disarmed principalities and powers, He made a public spectacle of them, triumphing over them in it" (Colossians 2:15).

Jesus, at His ascension, emptied paradise of the Old Testament saints and sealed up hell with its wicked forces.

Angels and demons

The good news for all of us is that there are two angels for every demon. They are often referred to as the angel armies. These faithful allies have been battle-tested and proven in the timeless ages of the past. Today angels stand with us to enforce the victory of the Son of God, while our defeated enemy is subject to all who believe in Christ. God will one day restore our planet, and a new Eden will be ours where together with the angels of glory we will glorify our Father and His Son, Jesus Christ!

Section Two

How **ANGELS** OPERATE

Chapter Seven

WORSHIP—
ANGELS
AROUND *the* THRONE

As allies with the angels, we cannot remain silent as
we experience the mighty works of God. We too must
shout His praises, for He is worthy!

O N MY FIRST MISSION TRIP TO HUEHUETENANGO,
Guatemala, I experienced angelic accompaniment in
worship. Hundreds of us were gathered in the convention center and had been worshiping through music and singing
for forty-five minutes when I noticed round orbs of light moving
overhead. I also heard sounds in addition to our voices and
instruments that were angelic in nature. In those moments I was

lifted into a deep intimacy with God; I began to cry, "Holy," and weep.

Angels are first and foremost worshipers of the living God! They were created to worship, as were we! Perhaps the oldest narrative in all Scripture is the Book of Job. In God's rebuke of Job, we catch a glimpse of the ancient past.

> Where were you when I laid the foundations of the earth? Tell Me, if you have understanding. Who determined its measurements? Surely you know! Or who stretched the line upon it? To what were its foundations fastened? Or who laid its cornerstone, when the morning stars sang together, and all the sons of God shouted for joy?
>
> —Job 38:4–7

Angels shouted as God the Father brought His creation into being. They were not silent observers of the great works of the Father; they responded with singing and shouting as His mighty power stretched into the vast universe.

Angels are first and foremost worshipers of the living God! They were created to worship, as were we!

Scripture enthusiastically accounts angels blessing and worshiping God our Father: "Bless the LORD, you His angels, who excel in strength, who do His word, heeding the voice of His word" (Psalm 103:20).

Angels are watching activities in the life of the church. First Timothy 5:21 lets us know that they will not operate when we violate what the Holy Spirit has charged us to do: "I charge you before God and the Lord Jesus Christ and the elect angels that you observe these things without prejudice, doing nothing with partiality."

CHURCH GATHERING AT THE END OF THE AGE

As we move toward the end of the age, angelic appearances will become more frequent. In Hebrews, there is a biblical picture of church gatherings that most of us have missed. I am convinced this describes worship shortly before Jesus comes to claim the church at the end. In our worship, the dimension of glory—the heavenlies—breaks through and commingles with us. Could it be that the scene described in Hebrews 12 is a picture of the church gathered on Earth rather than heaven?

> But you have come to Mount Zion and to the city of the living God, the heavenly Jerusalem, to an innumerable company of angels, to the general assembly and church of the firstborn who are registered in heaven, to God the Judge of all, to the spirits of just men made perfect, to Jesus the Mediator of the new covenant, and to the blood of sprinkling that speaks better things than that of Abel.
> —HEBREWS 12:22–24

True worship brings "the heavenly Jerusalem" to our gatherings. We are gathering with an "innumerable company of angels."

69

Note the following truths. First, the church will not be afraid of the manifest presence of God. When you read the record of Moses in Exodus 19, essentially the Israelites were afraid of God's presence. They had seen His mighty judgment on Egypt, and fear took hold of them. Many people today are afraid of God's powerful, glorious presence.

> Then it came to pass on the third day, in the morning, that there were thunderings and lightnings, and a thick cloud on the mountain; and the sound of the trumpet was very loud, so that all the people who were in the camp trembled. And Moses brought the people out of the camp to meet with God, and they stood at the foot of the mountain. Now Mount Sinai was completely in smoke, because the LORD descended upon it in fire. Its smoke ascended like the smoke of a furnace, and the whole mountain quaked greatly. And when the blast of the trumpet sounded long and became louder and louder, Moses spoke, and God answered him by voice.
>
> —EXODUS 19:16–19

God came down, but the people would not draw near. Notice it was the third day! This event was celebrated at the Feast of Pentecost. At this encounter they received the law but missed God's presence. They told Moses in essence, "Don't ever do this again!"

Another "third day" came fourteen hundred years later. As prophesied, on this third day Jesus rose from the dead. At the Feast of Pentecost, forty days later, God's power shook the earth again. This time the Spirit's manifestations were welcomed by the early church. Unfortunately many in the church today are afraid of God's presence.

True worship brings "the heavenly Jerusalem" to our gatherings. We are gathering with an "innumerable company of angels."

Look at this passage from Hebrews again and see what the End Time church gathering should look like: "But you have come to Mount Zion and to the city of the living God, the heavenly Jerusalem, to an innumerable company of angels" (Hebrews 12:22). Seven points were identified in Hebrews 12:22–27 that show us what the End Time church gatherings will look like. They are:

1. Angels gather with the kingdom church to give glory to God.

2. Intensified worship: Mount Zion was where David placed a choir and orchestra for thirty-three years, the length of Jesus's life on Earth. Their praise was offered continually. When the End Time church gathers, praise and worship go to the next level.

3. Innumerable angels join in the worship; in fact, there will be too many angels to count!

4. Worship breaking through to the other dimension and heaven kissing the church: The separation

between the spiritual realm and this world are blurred and breached in the kingdom church: "To the general assembly and church of the firstborn who are registered in heaven, to God the Judge of all, to the spirits of just men made perfect" (Hebrews 12:23).

5. God speaking a fresh word about the last days through the prophetic ministry: Angelic assistance will release the prophetic word to the End Time church. The kingdom church will experience direct revelation from heaven's mercy seat. Angels will watch over that word and release it through the church: "See that you do not refuse Him who speaks. For if they did not escape who refused Him who spoke on earth, much more shall we not escape if we turn away from Him who speaks from heaven" (Hebrews 12:25).

6. The church shaken to its foundations so that everything unnecessary is taken away: "Whose voice then shook the earth; but now He has promised, saying, 'Yet once more I shake not only the earth, but also heaven.' Now this, 'Yet once more,' indicates the removal of those things that are being shaken, as of things that are made, that the things which cannot be shaken may remain" (Hebrews 12:26–27).

7. The church receives kingdom truth and releases kingdom power to evangelize the End Time world.

Notice that all of this happens with the presence and assistance of an "innumerable company of angels." Understand this: we should expect and embrace more angelic contact in the last days. A shaking has already begun, and angel sightings are taking place where the kingdom is breaking through.

This should not surprise us since angels are always observed near the Old Testament temple worshiping continually. Since our bodies are the temples of the Holy Spirit, our hearts become the holy of holies when we enter into intimate worship. Angels are drawn to passionate worship. When we come together in the church assembly, we should be cognizant that these glorious beings who are older than time are gathering with us. They are still giving God all their worship! What angels did at the beginning they are still practicing eons later at the end of the age. They are praising God the Father and His Son, the Lord Jesus Christ. John describes a heavenly scene in Revelation 5 where he saw and heard the voice of many angels, living creatures, and the elders worshiping around the throne. In verse 11 he indicates this massive assembly was "ten thousand times ten thousand, and thousands of thousands." They worshiped with a loud voice.

As John Paul Jackson describes the scene in his book *7 Days Behind the Veil*, "The reason all Heaven keeps repeating, 'Holy, holy, holy,' is not because that's just what they do up there, strumming along with their little golden harps. 'Holy!' is a witness to what God has just done. Every time God acts, the act is holy, and so the angels and every other heavenly creature bear witness to that holy act and cry out 'Holy!'"[1]

*Since our bodies are the temples of the
Holy Spirit, our hearts become the holy of
holies when we enter into intimate worship.
Angels are drawn to passionate worship.*

As allies with the angels, we cannot remain silent as we experience the mighty works of God. We too must shout His praises, for He is worthy. If the angels, who are not recipients of the saving grace of Jesus Christ, never stop worshiping, how much more should we hasten to give Him all our praise!

Chapter Eight

DESTINY—

ANGELS

AMONG *the* NATIONS

Here we get a glimpse of the invisible war in the heavenly dimension. Intense warfare erupted in the heavenlies because one man with a prophetic calling prayed and fasted.

OUR LORD JESUS CHRIST WARNED THAT IN THE LAST days there would be "wars and rumors of wars." He also encouraged believers not to be afraid. He then said, "Nation will rise against nation, and kingdom against kingdom" (Matthew 24:6–7). Among the nations and kingdoms of the earth there will always be conflict. Hidden in these words of Jesus is the war between the dark forces of Satan and the angelic armies of Jesus.

As we move toward the end of the age, the sounds of war are being heard across our planet. Dark forces are drawing strength from false religions and are following demonic leadership toward the final conflagration on Earth. All roads lead toward the valley below the mountain of Megiddo, the place called Armageddon!

Islamic militants are receiving visits from the dark side instructing them in acts of terror, preparing for an all-out assault on the Jews and the nation of Israel. America and her allies are at war in the Middle East now and are searching for strategies to obstruct the purposes of darkness. As chaotic as the conflicts are on Earth, above the atmosphere of our planet, larger wars are raging. Here, our authentic allies, the angels, can and must be trusted. Daniel reveals the pattern of angelic operation among the nations.

Dark forces are drawing strength from false religions and are following demonic leadership toward the final conflagration on Earth.

Above every nation, Satan has assigned a "principality," and under that demon, "hosts of wickedness." Scripture affirms that there are evil demonic spirits over territories. Daniel rips the secrecy off this fact in his prophecy found in Daniel 10. Daniel had been fasting and mourning over captive Israel for three weeks. During that time of intense spiritual focus and physical deprivation Daniel received an angelic visit. That vision gives us some idea of what angels look like.

> Now on the twenty-fourth day of the first month, as I was by the side of the great river, that is, the Tigris, I lifted my eyes and looked, and behold, a certain man clothed in linen, whose waist was girded with gold of Uphaz! His body was like beryl, his face like the appearance of lightning, his eyes like torches of fire, his arms and feet like burnished bronze in color, and the sound of his words like the voice of a multitude.
>
> —DANIEL 10:4–6

This strong angel was brighter than lightning, glistening as fine jewels, and glowing as polished bronze. His words were as majestic as a waterfall. Daniel was the only one who saw the vision, however; as this magnificent scene unfolded, the men who were with him ran and hid in terror. They could sense the supernatural presence. Daniel was himself slain in the Spirit with his face to the ground as the angel spoke. The power of this supernatural encounter left him with no power in his flesh. He tells us that "suddenly, a hand touched me, which made me tremble on my knees and on the palms of my hands" (Daniel 10:10).

When the angel touched Daniel, he gained strength enough to get on all fours, in a reverential position, bowing down. His whole body trembled at the experience.

> And he said to me, "O Daniel, man greatly beloved, understand the words that I speak to you, and stand upright, for I have now been sent to you." While he was speaking this word to me, I stood trembling. Then he said to me, "Do not fear, Daniel, for

from the first day that you set your heart to understand, and to humble yourself before your God,
your words were heard; and I have come because
of your words. But the prince of the kingdom of
Persia withstood me twenty-one days; and behold,
Michael, one of the chief princes, came to help me,
for I had been left alone there with the kings of
Persia. Now I have come to make you understand
what will happen to your people in the latter days,
for the vision refers to many days yet to come."
—DANIEL 10:11–14

Daniel stood trembling to receive the prophetic word from the
angel. In the middle of this prophecy about "the latter days," the
angel spoke of warring with a territorial spirit called "the prince
of the kingdom of Persia." This demon was so strong that the
archangel Michael was summoned by God to rescue and release
the message.

Here we get a glimpse of the invisible war in the heavenly
dimension. Intense warfare erupted in the heavenlies because one
man with a prophetic calling prayed and fasted. However, this
demonic opposition resulted in a three-week delay in answer to
the prayer of Daniel. Note also that the struggle in this prophecy
was about Israel in the latter days! "Now I have come to make you
understand what will happen to your people in the latter days, for
the vision refers to many days yet to come" (Daniel 10:14).

It is a fact that we are living witnesses to that struggle. That
same demon of Persia is threatening Israel today. Behind every
earthly conflict is demonic influence. "The prince of Greece" is
also mentioned in this chapter: "Then he said, 'Do you know why
I have come to you? And now I must return to fight with the

prince of Persia; and when I have gone forth, indeed the prince of Greece will come'" (Daniel 10:20).

This is not simply a reference to the land of Greece. The spirit of Persia is the force behind Islam today, and this is a visible enemy that we battle alongside our angelic allies. The prince of Greece represents Greek philosophy that has captured and governs Western thought. Rationalism that denies the supernatural has taken over our educational system. Churches that deny the Holy Spirit's power have bowed to this "prince of Greece."

---

*Behind every earthly conflict
is demonic influence.*

This two-pronged enemy is arrayed against the Spirit-filled church today. The prince of Greece bows to the mind of man while the prince of Persia bows to a demon god. Can you see that the world conflict has clandestine operations going on in the spiritual realm? The prince, or spirit, of Greece (which is represented in the architecture of our government buildings in Washington DC) cannot defeat the Persian spirit. The church must rise to take down these spirits.

EXAMPLES OF ANGELIC INFLUENCE IN GOVERNMENT

There is a remarkable story in the Book of Judges when an angel comes to Manoah during a season of distress for the nation of Israel. God had allowed the Philistines to enslave the nation because they had done wrong. The angel came to prophesy the birth of Samson. Now Manoah's wife had been barren. This angel revealed his name to be "wonderful" (Judges 13:18). "Wonderful" comes from the Hebrew word *pala*, which is wonder worker or miracle worker. This angel called "wonderful" announced to Manoah and his barren wife that they would have a son named Samson who would deliver his nation from forty years of bondage! On a later occasion angels prophesied the death of Ahaziah through Elijah. Here was a regime-changing action initiated by angels. In this compelling story angels kill two captains of fifty with all their soldiers. The third captain begs for mercy, and a fearless Elijah issues the verdict of death to the wicked king. (See 2 Kings 1:1–17.)

In the New Testament an angel struck and killed King Herod when he tried to take God's glory for himself. Here again a national leader falls at the hand of an angel. In a later chapter you will see the increase of angelic operations among the nations at the end of the age. Angelic agents operate clandestinely among the nations of the earth. In a constant war with their demonic counterparts, angels affect the destiny of national and international governments.

Chuck Ripka, international banker, entrepreneur, marketplace minister, and author of *God Out of the Box*, shares a story about how he and the ministers of Elk River, Minnesota, were assisted by angels when the destiny of their state needed to be changed. As an ambassador of the kingdom, Chuck had received a specific word from God about the plans He had for bringing a revival to Minnesota. However, there were spiritual bondages that needed to be broken within the state legislature, so God sent them right to the source—the state capitol building—to begin the work through prayer. Chuck says:

When we were ready to step into the capitol, I sensed a strong demonic presence. I prayed, "Lord, would you please send warring angels to go into the capitol before us?"

Incredibly, I immediately saw two angels before me, each twenty feet tall. One had a sword, and the other had a huge hammer or mallet. They walked inside and caught a demon that looked like a Pan god from Greek mythology. It was half man and half animal. The angels bound the demon's hands, laid it on a block of granite, and then crushed its skull with the hammer.

As its head was being crushed, the hand of the demon opened up. A gold key fell to the ground.

The Lord said to me, "Now, with this key, no door will be locked to you."

We stepped inside…[and] the Lord began revealing to me what He wanted done that evening. "My heart grieves because there has been a separation between church and state," He said. "But My heart grieves even more because there has been a separation between church and church."[1]

In a constant war with their demonic counterparts, angels affect the destiny of national and international governments.

Chuck and this group of ministers proceeded to pray and repent for the sins the state and its constituents committed between racial groups, young against the old, and more. There was such a spirit of love and repentance in this meeting all because Chuck activated his authority and called on the angels of God to fight back the enemy and his attempts to cancel the movement of God in their state. Chuck reports that their "prayers and confessions had made a difference.... The atmosphere had changed. There was a new spirit of cooperation within the walls of the capitol. By following God's leading, we were able to help reconcile church and state *and* church and church."[2]

By understanding how angels interact with government in the spiritual realm, the believer's alliance with the angels becomes more important. The believer's worship, prayer, and witness can turn the tide in national and international struggle as demonstrated in Chuck's story. Had it not been for the release of those warring angels, he and his ministry team would have been up against enormous opposition to carry out God's plan for revival in Minnesota.

The believer's worship, prayer, and witness can turn the tide in national and international struggle.

In many respects, the church is viewed as a colony of the kingdom of heaven. Our role is to be ambassadors of the kingdom here on Earth. While loyal to our earthly nation and heritage, we must confess that we have a citizenship elsewhere. (See Philippians 3:20.) This concept elevates the gatherings of the people of God to cosmic and eternal importance. Jesus taught us to pray,

"Your kingdom come...on earth" (Matthew 6:10). In alliance with the triune God, His decrees, and the holy angels, we are a part of a destiny-changing enterprise.

Chapter Nine

PROTECTION—

ANGELS

on DEFENSE

There is a difference between invincibility and immunity. Invincibility means you can escape evil's trap. Immunity means that long before it gets to your borders, you'll know and you will be out of the way.

P SALM 34:7 SAYS, "THE ANGEL OF THE LORD ENCAMPS all around those who fear Him, and delivers them." And in Psalm 91:11 we read, "For He shall give His angels charge over you, to keep you in all your ways." God's angels guard and rescue all who reverence Him. The truth of this verse was made known in the life of the late Bill Bright, head of Campus Crusade for Christ, several years ago. His travels took him from continent to continent each year. He traveled in all kinds of circumstances and often faced danger. But he says that there was always peace in his heart that the Lord was with him. He knew he was surrounded by His guardian angels to protect him.

In Pakistan, during a time of great political upheaval, he had finished a series of meetings in Lahore and was taken to the train station. Though he was unaware of what was happening, an angry crowd of thousands was marching on the station to destroy it with cocktail bombs.

The director of the railway line rushed everyone onto the train, put each one in his compartment, and told them not to open the doors under any circumstances. The train ride to Karachi would require more than twenty-four hours, which was just the time Bill Bright needed to finish rewriting his book *Come Help Change the World.*

God sends His guardian angels to guard
and rescue those who reverence Him.

He recounts that he put on pajamas, reclined in the berth, and began to read and write. When the train arrived in Karachi twenty-eight hours later, he discovered how guardian angels had watched over and protected them all. The train in front of them had been burned when rioting students had lain on the track and refused to move. The train ran over the students. In retaliation, the mob burned the train and killed the officials.

Bill Bright was on the next train, and the rioters were prepared to do the same for that train. God miraculously went before the train and its passengers, and there were no mishaps. They arrived in Karachi to discover that martial law had been declared and all was peaceful. A Red Cross van took them to the hotel, and there God continued to protect them. When the violence subsided, Bill Bright was able to catch a plane for Europe. The scripture is true; God does send His guardian angels to guard and rescue those who reverence Him.[1]

There are angels that desire to release the benefits of the Lord to us. These angels do not bestow the gifts and protection of God, but they desire for us to join the Lord by getting into His presence, the secret place of the Most High. Angels worship in God's presence, and there we find their favor.

In biblical times, devout Jewish men worshiping in the temple wore a covering called a *tallith* or prayer shawl. This shawl was a private covering for the intercessors—a shield to symbolize they were spending intimate time alone with God. The tallith is still worn today.

That is what our secret place is like—a covering. King David wrote, "He who dwells in the secret place of the Most High shall abide under the shadow of the Almighty" (Psalm 91:1). We are to "abide" under the shadow of the Almighty. The word *abide* means "to tarry all night." It speaks of the intimacy of a husband and wife who tarry all night loving each other. When we abide in God's presence, the divine glory covers us, loves us, and hovers protectively over us.

Having entered into this close relationship with Jesus by trust, we become the beneficiaries of divine favor and enjoy protection by the angels.

A Place of Protection

Like a young eagle in its mother's nest, you are safe in His presence. His truth covers and protects you. "He shall cover you with His feathers, and under His wings you shall take refuge; His truth shall be your shield and buckler. You shall not be afraid of the terror by night" (Psalm 91:4–5).

Having entered into this close relationship with Jesus by trust, we become the beneficiaries of divine favor and enjoy protection by the angels.

Night terrors are a great problem with many today, children and adults alike. Fears of the dark remain with some youngsters well into their adult lives. Yet the unknown night stalkers of hell have no right when you are in that place of protection. No arrow of the wicked can penetrate the shield of faith and trust that guards the entrance to the secret place. In His presence, the old fears leave. While others may become victims of the enemy, you will be safe because of your close relationship to God.

Some years ago, a demented man approached me after a revival service in another city. He was about to hit me in the parking lot when Eddie Adams, my staff assistant, grabbed the man's arm. With his other hand, Eddie pushed me into the car and faced my attacker for me. That night, Eddie stood between my assailant and me. He was literally my shield!

If we abide in this place of protection, then we have Jesus and His angelic hosts present to step in for us to be our shield and our protection. Read this firsthand account by Mary Beth Barnes.

> I was preparing to go through the Seven Steps to Freedom, a deliverance and counseling ministry, and I found myself very afraid of the enemy. The enemy was telling me he wasn't going to leave me alone, nor was he going to allow me to be free. I knew I had to draw close to God and give Him my fears, or else I wouldn't be free from the hold Satan had on me. As I began to pray and tell God about the fear I had inside, I really entered into His presence. This is the scripture that the Holy Sprit gave me: "Because you have made the LORD, who is my refuge, even the Most High, your dwelling place, no evil shall befall you, nor shall any plague come near your dwelling; for He shall give His angels charge over you, to keep you in all your ways" (Psalm 91:9–11).
>
> As soon as the Holy Spirit ministered this scripture to me, I saw what seemed to be a black "glob" come out of the windows and every portal of my home; it then moved across my front yard and crossed to the other side of the road. When it was on the other side of the road it took on the shape of human-like "shadows," several dark figures.
>
> As I continued to watch these dark figures, suddenly I saw huge figures clothed in white standing about six feet apart all the way around the property line of my home. They seemed to stand at least ten feet tall with a very broad build and held in their right hands massive flaming swords. As

they stood at attention, their focus was on guarding my home and nothing more.

The black shadows tried to force themselves in between each angel but were only allowed to come as far as the angels were standing. It was as if they were hitting a piece of Plexiglas. They had absolutely no power against the authority that the angels were standing in. These angels didn't fight with them, nor did they struggle with the black shadows; they simply stood guard with the flaming swords around my "dwelling place."

On a final note, the Lord has "kept me in all my ways" and propelled me into a fearless life of freedom through the power of His Holy Spirit.

There is a place where neither devil nor disease can disturb our walk or destroy our witness for Jesus. You see, we go because of His strength! We actually carry His dwelling with us! Angels watch over our every step.

No arrow of the wicked can penetrate the shield of faith and trust that guards the entrance to the secret place.

Here is another story a man named Al shared about how he as a young child was saved by an angel from certain death. He was born at 4:02 a.m. in Jersey City, New Jersey. His mother and father were on their way to the hospital when they were hit head-on by another car.

His father suffered two broken legs, and his mother was far worse. She was severely injured from the waist down and from the sternum up. She was given her last rites at the scene. Miraculously, she survived, but she spent the next seventeen months in the hospital; Al's grandmother took care of him during that time.

Exactly one year to the day later, baby Al was sleeping in his grandmother's house. It was a beautiful fall evening. The windows were open, and his grandmother had a religious candle on a dresser.

The wind kicked up just enough to blow the sheer drapes near the candle flame. The house caught fire, and his nursery was engulfed in flames. The fireman who eventually rescued baby Al could not believe his eyes (according to the fireman and conversations years later). The fireman stated that when he entered the nursery through the smoke and heat, two large angels were crouched over the baby's bed. He said he froze for a moment, and all of a sudden this one big angel with a trumpet around his body picked up baby Al and handed the baby to the fireman. Not a scratch was on the baby, and there was no lung damage from smoke inhalation either. Both his birth and his escaping the fire were called miracles of God by the local newspapers and the local television stations. He is living proof that angels exist and come to a child's aid.[2]

Someone had prayed over baby Al to be protected during all the turmoil surrounding his birth and early childhood. They must have known God's heart for children and that children have angels assigned to assist and protect them. Matthew 18:10 says, "Take heed that you do not despise one of these little ones, for I say to you that in heaven their angels always see the face of My Father who is in heaven." This verse shows that angels are assigned to children at birth, yet they watch and wait for God's instruction to assist them. Parents and leaders, like those in Al's life, have authority to invoke angelic protection over their children and others. But there is an order to how angels operate and how we are able to have maximum angelic protection.

ANGELIC PROTOCOL

Angels operate, as we have learned, on divine protocol. They are creatures of order and discipline. More often than not, we desire to skip a step and get our miracle or breakthrough instantly. But there are three important levels to climb before God will release increase. Psalm 91 gives the protocol for increase.

> *Parents and leaders have authority to invoke angelic protection over their children and others.*

1. Intimacy—moving to safer ground

The first key to victory is intimacy with God: "He who dwells in the secret place of the Most High shall abide under the shadow of the Almighty. I will say of the LORD, 'He is my refuge and my fortress; my God, in Him I will trust'" (Psalm 91:1–2).

If you are going to avoid evil, you must have an intimate relationship with Jesus Christ. Likewise, if you desire to obey the commands of Christ, you must abide in Him. In just the first two verses of Psalm 91, we find four different names of God. Our Maker wants us to know His name, to know His very character.

How do you get into God's presence and abide there? Here is the golden gateway into God's presence: "I will say of the LORD, 'He is my refuge and my fortress; my God, in Him I will trust'" (Psalm 91:2).

You see, God inhabits praise! When we begin to audibly confess His Word out of our mouth, when we extol His might and power, then we discover the place of intimacy with Him. You move into what the psalmist David called the secret place of the Most High, an open door to His presence.

When you look at Psalm 91:1–2, you know God desires our love! Everything flows from God when we have a passionate love for Him.

2. Invincibility—the first line of defense

This psalm moves you from intimacy to a new level of protection, I believe, provided by angels.

> Surely He shall deliver you from the snare of the fowler and from the perilous pestilence. He shall cover you with His feathers, and under His wings you shall take refuge; His truth shall be your shield and buckler. You shall not be afraid of the terror by night, nor of the arrow that flies by day, nor of the pestilence that walks in darkness, nor of the destruction that lays waste at noonday. A thousand may fall at your side, and ten thousand at your right hand; but it shall not come near you. Only with your eyes shall you look, and see the reward of the wicked.
>
> —PSALM 91:3–8

Once you've come to a place of complete oneness, you move on to a place of invincibility. Psalm 91 tells us that in the safety of the shadow of His presence we will escape many traps of the enemy and that God will "deliver you from the snare of the fowler" (verse 3). In biblical times, a snare containing a lure or bait was used to catch birds or animals. The devil sets dangerous traps for believers, but those who are walking, talking, and speaking forth who Jesus is will be delivered from these traps, including traps of deception, doubt, darkness, demonic forces, disease, disasters, and defeat.

If you are hearing from God and walking with Him on a daily basis, it doesn't mean that disasters won't happen. It doesn't mean the disease doesn't come; it simply means that those things cannot deter you from Christ. Here is a guarantee of victory. Your eyes will see as God walks you through the battlefields of life with complete victory!

Let me share with you a story that was reported on *FOX and Friends* news show on Christmas Day in 2008. Angels and Christmas seem to go together. During Christmas week in 2008, Chelsea was about to die of pneumonia. The fourteen-year-old girl was about to be taken off life support when Dr. Teresa Sunderland saw an angelic image at the door of the pediatric intensive care unit. The bright white image was caught on a security camera. It couldn't have been a strange light as there are no windows in that part of the building. Dr. Ophelia Garmon-Brown of the hospital declares it a Christmas miracle. By the way, Chelsea recovered immediately and came home for Christmas.[3] Angels help in healing.

The devil sets dangerous traps for believers, but those who are walking, talking, and speaking forth who Jesus is will be delivered from these traps, including traps of deception, doubt, darkness, demonic forces, disease, disasters, and defeat.

---

3. Immunity—the deepest level of protection

There is a difference between invincibility and immunity. Invincibility means you can escape evil's trap. Immunity means that long before it gets to your borders, you'll know and you will be out of the way. Immunity means that instead of a fight, there is a place where demonic forces cannot go. God provides seasons of rest from the struggle. Notice again that the key is intimacy. Everything begins with intimate worship. The psalmist refers back to making the Lord one's dwelling: "Because you have made the LORD, who is my refuge, even the Most High, your dwelling place" (Psalm 91:9).

At the place of immunity there are four things that start happening.

1. *Accidents stop happening!* "No evil shall befall you" (verse 10). All of a sudden tires do not go flat, appliances do not tear up, falls that break bones stop, and cars do not hit your car. There is a place of immunity.

2. *Sicknesses stop spreading!* "Nor shall any plague come near your dwelling" (verse 10). How would you like to get through winter without colds and flu ravaging your family?

3. *Angels start helping!* Angels operate most effectively when you are intimate with the Lord Jesus. Your house becomes protected when you have made Him your dwelling! Angels will even keep you from tripping over a rock! "In their hands they shall bear you up, lest you dash your foot against a stone" (verse 12).

4. *Devils start losing!* What was once over your head is now trampled under your feet! "You shall tread upon the lion and the cobra, the young lion and the serpent you shall trample underfoot" (verse 13). Angels will warn you and protect you from all that the enemy may try to bring against you. In many respects, it's just like a warning before a tsunami.

Millions of dollars have been spent placing tsunami-warning systems on the Indian Ocean following the devastation that hit in December 2004. These new devices are ultrasensitive, sending a split-second signal to a satellite if the ocean rises even a foot and warning affected countries within moments of detection. This reminds us of the power of our connection with God, for His warning system gives us notice and reports long before evil can come to hinder our path! His warning agents are the angels!

---

*God has made you significant and
special because you love Him.*

In the historic home of John Wesley, the great Methodist, there is a very small upstairs room. This space was his prayer room that he used daily at 4:30 a.m. No wonder so many hymns, so much ministry, and so much anointing flowed out of Wesley. He had an appointment with God at 4:30 each morning! As a result, the promise of Psalm 91:9–10 was his.

God's promise is to "set you on high" because you "set your love on Him." To be set on high indicates honor, to be made excellent, to be shown and proclaimed as special! God has made you significant and special because you love Him.

Psalm 91:14–15 reveals clear promises to those who dwell in His presence, love His name, and have no desire but to know Him better.

- *I will deliver him.* This means the enemy will never hold you in sin's spiritual prison!

- *I will set him on high.* God will take care of your reputation. Let promotion come from the Lord.

- *He shall call upon Me, and I will answer.* God will always answer your prayers.

- *I will be with him in trouble.* This promise assures you that you never will face anything alone! In Matthew 28:20, Jesus said, "Lo, I am with you always, even to the end of the age."

 I will honor him. Only the applause of heaven really matters. His "well done" is enough.

 With long life I will satisfy him. God will extend your days so that you will live a satisfied, full, and overflowing life and will leave this life with blazing energy across the finish line!

 I will show him My salvation. The word for "salvation" in this passage is *Yeshua*, which is Hebrew for Jesus! Thus, the best promise is saved for last—God will show you Jesus! To see Jesus is the beginning and end of everything.

SOMETHING ABOUT THAT NAME

There is just something about the name Jesus! His name is power, and within the folds of its protection, believers can know a secret place where there is anointing, safety, and blessing—a tower of strength that keeps us from evil! Our planet has become "the killing fields" of hell, yet we can live, at times, immune to all these plagues.

There is such significance in knowing God's name. This "knowing" means much more than head knowledge; it refers to the closest possible intimacy. To know God's name is to be completely broken, having learned all the secrets and nuances of His character. The name of Jesus encompasses so much! Look at a few of the names of God:

 Yahweh—the Great I Am
 Jireh—my Provider
 Tsidkenu—my Righteousness
 Rophe—my Healer

- Rohi—my Shepherd
- Nissi—my Leader and Lover
- Shalom—my Peace
- Shammah—my Companion

Yes, He is also our Christ, the Anointed One, and the Messiah of the world. He is wonderful! He is our Lord! He is before the beginning and after the end! He is the unceasing song of David resounding across time and all of creation! He is the ever-shining star that will never fade. Angels move on behalf of those who know God's names!

Christ Jesus is the One we meet in that secret place. It is His scarred hand that takes us up and His shining face that welcomes us in. There we will whisper the name of Jesus and find ourselves abiding in the Almighty, overwhelmed with the promise and blessing of His presence! And there the angels will cover us.

Chapter Ten

GUIDANCE—

OUT FRONT

Angelic intermediaries are often used by God to get God's people from one place to another. Sometimes they simply give direction, and the believer must, by faith, obey.

ANGELS MIRACULOUSLY DIRECT AND PROTECT GOD'S people. Listen to Jacob Lepard's record of an angelic direction given to a group from our church while on a mission trip in Brazil.

In June of 2005, the summer before my senior year, a group of thirteen students from our church, two parent chaperones, and our youth minister were given the opportunity to take a mission trip to Castanhal in northern Brazil. We were to be gone for ten days, spending most of our time in the city working and living with a local pastor and his family. The rest of the time we spent traveling on the Moju River, which is an offshoot of the Amazon, helping with their church-planting ministry. After we had been in Castanhal for about five days, we packed our things and boarded a bus that took us out of the city to a dock near the highway, where we met the boat that would take us up the river. We were told the area where we met the boat was considerably dangerous, as several robberies had occurred there recently. However, like nearly all threats in Brazil, it was only dangerous at night, so this time around we were safe.

Our plans for the second day out on the river were to hike from early afternoon till evening several miles into the rain forest to a village where the missionary would speak at the village church. The boat was to drop us off at the trailhead and continue down the river to meet a van that would transport the missionary, the pastor, and their families to the village. The plan was for us all to load up in the van and return to our boat by road after the church service, but we were in for a surprise. We began the hike apprehensively, having been told countless stories about the local wildlife but all the time being reassured that none of the aggressive animals came out until nightfall, long after we would arrive at the village. As the hike continued, our apprehension evolved into extreme desire to not contract a jungle parasite as our trail turned from packed dirt to rotted planks suspended above swampy wetland. Needless to say I spent far more time in the mud than on the eight-inch wide trail. This occurred for two reasons: (1) I didn't listen to my mother when she told me a foundation in gymnastics would help me later in life, and (2) the rotted planks had a tendency to bend or break under the weight of a healthy American. Regardless, right at sunset, after about two and a half hours of hiking, we emerged muddy and tired from the forest but steeped in a sense of accomplishment and respect for people who made the trip daily.

Shortly after arriving at the village we received news that the missionary, pastor, and their families had not arrived as they were supposed to, and nobody knew when they would arrive with the van. We wouldn't find out until much later that night that they had been late in meeting the van, and as a result the impatient driver had simply left. Consequently, at the exact moment that we arrived at the village, they were hitchhiking their way up the highway in a beer truck with a driver who never said a word, only smiling and giving aid when it was absolutely needed.

In looking back on that night I understand why it was so full of spiritual warfare. There are a lot of details that I could share about the service, but what moved me the most is how powerfully God moved and how unexpectedly He did it. The church was a small 30 x 30 building lit by a single light bulb connected to a car battery, and every believer from the surrounding area, probably two hundred in all, was crammed in.

In the absence of the expected missionary, our youth minister got up and spoke via translator about what was on his heart, consisting mainly of the truth of the cross and the reality of grace. At the end of the short message several people received salvation, after which nearly everyone came forward to be prayed over for healing. This last part caught all of us by surprise. I can say for sure that God was present and that He was fulfilling promises and healing His people when there were no doctors for hundreds of miles. I am astounded by what He did and the way He moved during the service. In looking back, I know that this was the reason that we were supposed to be there and the reason why we were under such heavy attack from the enemy.

By the end of the service it was well past the planned leaving time, and the others had finally been able to reach us, only to inform us that there was no van and we would have to hike back through the rain forest. The prospect of a night hike had been in the back of our minds the entire time, knowing full well that the already low chances of staying out of the mud during the day would be greatly reduced by darkness, not to mention fear of large snakes. But because we had no other option, we trusted that God would make a way. We began quoting Psalm 91 and started walking back toward the trail. Probably no more than fifty feet from the trailhead we heard somebody shouting for us to stop and go to the road instead, that there was someone waiting for us there. Not fully understanding, we walked a quarter of a mile to the deserted highway where we found an air-conditioned city transport bus waiting with the engine idling. God had made a way out, which was undeniably His doing.

We boarded the bus and found the driver sitting in the back. When we asked why he was there, his only reply was that he had been told to wait there until people arrived, never offering any more explanation than that. He drove us all the way back to the dock, where we had originally boarded the day before, in silence. There we would wait on the boat to receive word of where we were and travel downriver to pick us up. We sat together in a circle, waiting by the river and watching clouds gather overhead that signified the Amazon rainy season. All the time that we sat there in the dark, the bus driver stood alone just outside of our circle, in many ways seeming to be standing guard. As I said, we'd been told the place was very dangerous at night.

Because we had no other option, we trusted that God would make a way.

After a comparatively short wait the boat arrived, and just as the last person had gotten under the shelter of the boat, the storm hit like a tidal wave. I looked back at the riverbank and saw the bus pulling back onto the highway. I had not gotten the chance to say a word to the silent bus driver the entire night, but I've given him much thought since then. To be honest, I can't say whether he or the beer truck driver were man or angel, but I can tell the story, and I know for a fact that there was unseen opposition to the movement of God that night in the rain forest. Despite this, our God was present powerfully, faithful in fulfilling His word to believers, and, even more, was glorified. This tells me there also had to be unseen allies, and in two possible cases ones that took physical form.

The truth is no one knows who sent the bus, who paid for the bus, or why it was there. Did angels direct that bus to them? Was the driver an angel? I know our thirteen young people were protected and delivered out of the Amazon jungle by angels.

Angelic intermediaries are often used by God to get God's people from one place to another. Sometimes they simply give direction, and the believer must, by faith, obey. Such an event took place in the life of Paul when he was making his final journey to Rome. Strangely the angel could not stop the ship-wreck because the sailors had already violated the laws of sailing during that season. Despite Paul's warning that the voyage would end with disaster with loss of the cargo and ship and also their lives, the captain set sail. Still Paul fasted and prayed. Soon the winds arose, the ship was battered, and when impending disaster loomed near, Paul said:

> Men, you should have listened to me, and not have sailed from Crete and incurred this disaster and loss. And now I urge you to take heart, for there will be no loss of life among you, but only of the ship. For there stood by me this night an angel of the God to whom I belong and whom I serve, saying, "Do not be afraid, Paul; you must be brought before Caesar;

and indeed God has granted you all those who sail
with you."

—Acts 27:21–24

Because of Paul's fasting and prayer, an angel came and granted Paul the lives of all on board. Even when we make unwise decisions, angels will bring wisdom to deliver. You may be the beneficiary of the angels watching over someone else whom you have led into a mess. If you are in a storm not of your own making, cry out to God! He will send His angels to direct you.

Another notable example is Lot, who, along with his family, was warned of impending judgment. It is interesting to notice the ministry of these angels to Lot. First of all, they were visible: "Now the two angels came to Sodom in the evening, and Lot was sitting in the gate of Sodom. When Lot saw them, he rose to meet them, and he bowed himself with his face toward the ground" (Genesis 19:1).

---

*If you are in a storm not of your
own making, cry out to God! He
will send His angels to direct you.*

Most of us have never seen angels with our physical eyes; however, Scripture is filled with angelic appearances. In the case of Lot, not only did he see them, but he also approached them. And if this divine intersect was not dramatic enough, Lot actually invited them to his house and offered to wash their feet: "Here now, my lords, please turn in to your servant's house and spend the night, and wash your feet; then you may rise early and go on your way.' And they said, 'No, but we will spend the night in the open square'" (verse 2).

The angels wouldn't let Lot wash their feet, but they did eat the feast that he prepared: "But he insisted strongly; so they turned in to him and entered his house. Then he made them a feast, and baked unleavened bread, and they ate" (verse 3).

They were physically attractive and looked like men.

> Now before they lay down, the men of the city, the men of Sodom, both old and young, all the people from every quarter, surrounded the house. And they called to Lot and said to him, "Where are the men who came to you tonight? Bring them out to us that we may know them carnally."
>
> —GENESIS 19:4–5

Sodom was a corrupt and immoral society. These angels were not only visible but also attractive to the lost men of that city. They did not respect the holy state of these spiritual beings. In fact, they lusted after them. These angels also had supernatural power: "And they struck the men who were at the doorway of the house with blindness, both small and great, so that they became weary trying to find the door.... 'For we will destroy this place, because the outcry against them has grown great before the face of the LORD, and the LORD has sent us to destroy it'" (verses 11, 13).

These angels were there to exact judgment on the city. However, they were subject to the needs of Lot; they served Lot: "'Hurry, escape there. For I cannot do anything until you arrive there.' Therefore the name of the city was called Zoar" (verse 22).

In my own life I have received direction from angels. In 1978 I was in my eighteenth day of ministry in the village of Mingading on the island of Mindanao, Philippines, when suddenly during the service an earthquake caused all in attendance to flee the building. Later that evening I could hear gunfire, and in the middle of the night I was awakened by an English-speaking person. It was obvious that my interpreter had fled with all his belongings, and the soldiers assigned to protect me were nowhere to be found. The one who awakened me said, "Get all your things together and be ready to leave." While I packed my belongings, this stranger disappeared. As I stepped out of the bamboo hut, I saw headlights coming up the mountain road. To my relief, it was a jeep with a female American missionary. The same "English-speaking person" had instructed her in the middle of the night to leave M'lang and come to Mingading to help someone in need. I left with her and went to the Baptist Mission Compound in M'lang. The next morning "Moros," Muslim rebels, came to the village of Mingading looking for the American. I firmly believe an angel intervened.

Chapter Eleven

STRENGTH—

PLUGGED IN

Angels do not strengthen one simply because he or she is tired; they are available to those on kingdom assignments.

THREE DAYS AND NIGHTS HAD PASSED WITH NO SLEEP following the birth of our second daughter. Still a seminary student, I served as a full-time pastor and was on my way to church with my head still buzzing from lack of sleep. I had scribbled an outline and a few thoughts on paper but felt exhausted and inadequate.

As I entered my small study and closed the door, a feeling of utter aloneness swept over me. With a knock on the door, Dave Davidson brought in a cup of steaming, hot coffee and a big, fresh doughnut.

"How are you, preacher?" he asked. I fell into his arms in exhaustion. Dave said, "I know you're tired, but God's angels will strengthen you!"

At exactly 11:20 that morning as I rose to preach, a warmth and strength flowed through my body and my spirit. Dave was so right! The angels came and strengthened me.

Angels are here to strengthen believers who have an intimate relationship with Jesus Christ. Angels will not do for us what we have been asked to do. They can, however, strengthen us for our assignments. Because we need the strength given us by angels, it causes us to face our own inadequacies. Often we find ourselves weary and worn out from the daily struggles of life. Fatigue is a first cousin to depression. Satan's goal is to cause us to quit! The Word of God says that in the last days Satan's emissaries will try to "wear out the saints of the most High" (Daniel 7:25, KJV). Life at its best can be a wearisome experience; however, God makes provision for our strength.

ELIJAH STRENGTHENED

The prophet Elijah had won a great victory over the forces of darkness. In the Super Bowl of spiritual warfare, Elijah had called down fire from heaven and exposed the false prophets of Baal. Elijah defeated those prophets and turned the people back to the one true God. With that battle won and the three-and-a-half-year drought broken, revival came to the land. There was no rest for the prophet, however.

Queen Jezebel made Elijah number one on her hit list and pursued him. Elijah fled until exhausted, and he sat under a "broom tree." As depression took over, Elijah wished he could die. Scripture records this marvelous story of angelic assistance as Elijah received a touch and food from an angel. In fact, the angel baked him a cake that gave him forty days of strength. (See 1 Kings 19:6–8.)

DANIEL STRENGTHENED

We find once again in Scripture the story of the prophet Daniel, who also received strength from an angel. Daniel was so overwhelmed by all God had revealed to him, he almost died. But the angel came and touched Daniel. Then the angel gave him a word from the Lord. Both the touch and the word gave Daniel strength for his assignment. (See Daniel 10:17–19.)

THE LORD JESUS STRENGTHENED

On two occasions we find our Lord receiving strength from the angels. At His temptation in the wilderness, Jesus encountered strength-sapping temptation from Satan. Remember, as we discussed earlier, Satan's goal is to "wear out" the believer. In the wilderness, Satan attacked Jesus with a threefold blow, testing His resolve. Jesus defeated Satan by answering every test with the Word of God. When the battle was over, the angels came. "Then the devil left Him, and behold, angels came and ministered to Him" (Matthew 4:11).

As our Lord faced the dreadful cup of our sins in the Garden of Gethsemane, He looked into that cup and shrank from it in horror. Yet in the end, Jesus drank its awful potion to the last dregs. How was Jesus able to face that horrible assignment? An angel came from glory to help Him: "Then an angel appeared to Him from heaven, strengthening Him" (Luke 22:43). Jesus Christ did not avoid the inevitable cup but was strengthened for the task by the angel.

HOW BELIEVERS ARE STRENGTHENED BY ANGELS

Even in contemporary times, God's angels still come to strengthen believers during difficult times. A young man shares a story about when he had trouble recovering from surgery and an angel came to his aid. He recalls:

> I required knee surgery a few years ago; I prayed a lot before surgery asking God to guide the hands of all those in the theatre and to bring me safely out of the anesthetic. I apparently inhaled too deeply the anesthetic and had a hard time coming back into consciousness.
>
> I remember being very frightened, as I did not want to die—I had so much more to live for. Immediately, a white light appeared and a voice encouraged me. It said, "Breathe, breathe, you can do it, you will come out of the anesthetic. Do not fight it."
>
> I know it was an angel of God speaking to me, so I can attest to angels being present all the time and having us always in their care. I have experienced it.
>
> Thank God for His angels![1]

Observing this story and the biblical antecedents presented in the previous section, we see some ways we may receive strength from the angels. Make note and remember the following:

1. Angels strengthen those on serious assignment from God. Angels do not strengthen one simply because he or she is tired; they are available to those on kingdom assignments.

2. The presence of angels releases a measure of strength. The word *appear* means to bring the assistance of one's presence. As a young boy I was threatened by a bully five years older than me. One day the bully beat me. My mother sent her younger brother with me to avenge my beating. My uncle took care of that bully! Even though I did not strike a blow, I felt strong! I was strong in my uncle's presence! When he appeared, all my weakness left. Likewise, angelic appearance routs demonic strength killers.

3. Angels touch and minister to weak believers. The brush of an angel's wing can strengthen the believer for their journey.

4. Angels speak the Word of God, and believers are strengthened by the word of angels. God will send us a hopeful, faithful message through the angels that will strengthen and prepare us for what lies ahead.

5. Angels can cook and feed believers. With this, we see angels can use tangible items to bring strength

to the body and soul of a believer, or many times angels will use people to provide the necessities that strengthen the believer.

6. Angels can transport believers on occasion, as we see the deacon Philip whisked away from Samaria by an angel (Acts 8:26–40). Angels can carry us when we are too tired in our own strength and can lift us up to keep us from tripping over a stone (Psalm 91).

To summarize, angels are available to strengthen us along the way. As we see in Revelation 5:2, which speaks of a "strong angel," the word *strong* translates to mean "force, innate power." In essence, strong angels are with us to strengthen us.

Section Three

How

ANGELS

ARE ACTIVATED

Chapter Twelve

OBEY ORDERS

"We have walked to and fro throughout the earth, and behold, all the earth is resting quietly" (Zechariah 1:11).

NGELS ARE ASSIGNED THE RESPONSIBILITY TO SERVE believers. When a believer operates as an heir to the kingdom of God, then angels are sent to serve. Our failure to activate angelic assistance has limited our growth and success in our mission enterprise. There is a powerful word on angels found in Hebrews 1:14. It says, "Are they not all ministering spirits sent forth to minister for those who will inherit salvation?" The phrase "sent forth" is the Greek word *apostello*, which is the same word translated as "apostle." Angels are "sent forth" with those who are willing to "go forth." The phrase "sent forth" means to be sent out with a commission. Angels protect and endorse the message God is speaking today by using their authority. The phrase also speaks of the apostolic, prophetic, and evangelistic work done as they help the spread the good news.

> *Angels go before us on life's journey*
> *toward our promised destiny.*

ANGELS GIVE INSTRUCTIONS

I had just turned twenty-one years old and was experiencing one of the most exciting times in my young life. I was newly married, a student at Samford University and had just begun a new ministry at a church in Wilsonville, Alabama. As I drove to Birmingham for a long day of classes, I noticed a young man hitchhiking. Normally, I never stop for hitchhikers; however, on this day I stopped for the young man.

As I watched him get in my car, he said, "Now worship Jesus Christ."

Then he said, "I must tell you something. You will have an awakening, and you will baptize dozens of people. Do not be dismayed if the old church does not receive all that God releases. You are appointed here for the purpose of touching the people no one wants."

He then asked me to let him out of the car. As he got out of the car, I said, "God bless you."

He looked at me, smiled, and said, "He already has, and He has blessed you!"

Two weeks later we baptized thirty-six new converts; most of them lived in a poor community of small shotgun houses. The church did not receive them, but God put a love in my heart, from that moment until now, for the needy and outcast. I believe I encountered an angel.

Angels go before us on life's journey toward our promised destiny. In Exodus 33:2, God said, "And I will send My Angel before you, and I will drive out the Canaanite and the Amorite and the Hittite and the Perizzite and the Hivite and the Jebusite." It is comforting to know that the Lord is directing our way and that His angels take each step before us. There are angelic "scouts" exploring and preparing the way ahead.

ANGELS WARN BELIEVERS

Remember, the angel warned Joseph of Herod's evil intention: "Now when they had departed, behold, an angel of the Lord appeared to Joseph in a dream, saying, 'Arise, take the young Child and His mother, flee to Egypt, and stay there until I bring you word; for Herod will seek the young Child to destroy Him'" (Matthew 2:13). Throughout history angels have waved red flags in front of believers, and we can count on that same protective intervention in our lives today.

Bart was on his way to Branson, Missouri, for the annual Yamaha motorcycle convention when he had an unbelievable encounter that he will never forget. He was traveling on his motorcycle behind a semitruck, going seventy to seventy-five miles an hour when he heard a clear voice inside of him say, "Switch lanes to the left."

As soon as he had completed the lane change, the semitrailer in front of him blew a rear tire and scattered large pieces of tread in the right lane, where he had been just moments before. Bart honestly believes that if it were not for that divine intervention telling him to switch lanes, he would not be alive today. He probably would have crashed into the back of the semi or flipped the bike after hitting the separated tread.

That day Bart is sure that he heard his angel tell him, clear as a bell, to switch lanes because there was trouble ahead.[1]

ANGELS ARE WATCHING

When we bind the enemy and loose our allies, the angels do the work for us. Many times the church, collectively and as individuals, does not stand on our position in Christ. As a result, we fail to engage the legions of angels standing ready to assist. Matthew 16:19 puts it like this: "And I will give you the keys of the kingdom of heaven, and whatever you bind on earth will be bound in heaven, and whatever you loose on earth will be loosed in heaven." As believers operate, they must understand that angelic assistance is a "key" to kingdom power in the earth. These wonderful beings are the agents of God who operate in opening doors and binding the curses.

The mighty hosts of heaven are called "watchers" in Scripture. I am convinced that angels can reveal international crises and international needs. As "watchers," they are looking out for all believers! Angels are God's scouts on the earth doing reconnaissance. In Zechariah chapter 1, we find the angels walking to and fro, or to put it in more contemporary language, walking back and forth throughout the earth keeping watch over creation. This night they had a good report: "We have walked to and fro throughout the earth, and behold, all the earth is resting quietly" (Zechariah 1:11).

The prophet Daniel also calls angels "watchers." They are doing surveillance over all creation. Above our earth are man-made satellites recording global activities; in a greater way, angels are also watching over us. "I saw in the visions of my head while on my bed, and there was a watcher, a holy one, coming down from heaven" (Daniel 4:13).

As believers operate, they must understand that angelic assistance is a "key" to kingdom power in the earth.

I was chatting with my recently widowed mother-in-law, a faithful Christian, about living alone. She has opted to stay in the large house where she and my father-in-law, Billy, had lived so long. She quickly told me she was not afraid. With a shy smile, she said, "I know that angels are watching over me."

When Billy was in his last living moments, there in their home with all the family gathered around, he opened his blue eyes and looked heavenward as a glory filled the room. Billy then closed his eyes and went to heaven. Though not visible, an angel had come to transport him home to glory, and I firmly believe angels have stayed with my mother-in-law, Polly, ever since.

Angels are always on guard, covering the earth. They report on all that they observe on the earth. If we are on the right channel, we too can have wisdom on what God is doing in the earth.

Chapter Thirteen

RESPOND
to SCRIPTURE

When a faithful Christian says aloud the Word God
has released in him or her, that Word is carried forth
on the wings of angels to be answered.

F OR THIRTY YEARS I HAVE SERVED AS PASTOR OF ABBA'S
House. During that time I have prepared and delivered
over five thousand messages, which totals over sixty-
five thousand written pages. I have written seventeen books
and have taught daily radio for over ten of those years, which
equal more than three thousand messages. During all this time,
I can honestly say that most people who heard these scriptural

messages didn't respond. However, it is encouraging to know that not a single angel disobeyed the Word of God that came forth from my mouth.

Angels are activated by the Word of God and move accordingly. They don't do as we humans sometimes do—respond to God's commands reluctantly or depending on how we feel about what He is asking. When God speaks, they act. Angels reverence, respect, and respond to the Word of God. They have a special interest in presenting, protecting, proclaiming, and performing the Word of God. Angels will not violate the written Word of God; they are committed to its dictates. In most cases when angelic involvement occurs, a message from heaven is being delivered. Angels know that the messages they deliver change the destiny of nations and are of life-and-death importance.

ANGELS AND THE ORIGIN OF SCRIPTURE

Scripture speaks of their heavenly origin. Scripture is the God-breathed writings of men giving witness to the mighty acts of God: "All Scripture is given by inspiration of God, and is profitable for doctrine, for reproof, for correction, for instruction in righteousness" (2 Timothy 3:16).

In this verse, Paul declares the writings of the Bible to be God breathed. The Holy Spirit actively superintended the writing of Scripture. Simon Peter affirmed that Scripture came from God to humanity: "And so we have the prophetic word confirmed, which you do well to heed as a light that shines in a dark place, until the day dawns and the morning star rises in your hearts; knowing this first, that no prophecy of Scripture is of any private interpretation, for prophecy never came by the will of man, but holy men of God spoke as they were moved by the Holy Spirit" (2 Peter 1:19–21).

> *Angels are activated by the Word*
> *of God and move accordingly.*
> *When God speaks, they act.*

Beyond the connection between God and man, we find an ally in the formation of Scripture, the holy angels. The angels were deeply involved in the giving of the Word. When Moses ascended Mount Sinai, he was met by an innumerable company of angels, who participated in the revelation of the Law: "And he said: 'The LORD came from Sinai, and dawned on them from Seir; He shone forth from Mount Paran, and He came with ten thousands of saints; from His right hand came a fiery law for them" (Deuteronomy 33:2). The word *saints* is "holy ones," and scholars agree that it is a reference to angels.[1]

Psalm 68:17 affirms the angelic covering at Mount Sinai when Moses conferred with God about the Law that would become the bedrock of human civilization: "The chariots of God are twenty thousand, even thousands of thousands; the Lord is among them as in Sinai, in the Holy Place."

When you turn to the pages of the New Testament, you find a clear affirmation of angelic assistance with the Scriptures, especially the Law. The deacon Stephen, in his sermon that resulted in his martyrdom, declared the same truth: "...who have received the law by the direction of angels and have not kept it" (Acts 7:53).

The Law came "by the direction of the angels." The apostle Paul, in writing to the Galatian church, said the Law was "appointed" by angels: "What purpose then does the law serve? It was added because of transgressions, till the Seed should come to whom the promise was made; and it was appointed through angels by the hand of a mediator" (Galatians 3:19).

Furthermore, the writer of Hebrews declares the absolute integrity of the "word spoken through angels": "For if the word spoken through angels proved steadfast, and every transgression and disobedience received a just reward..." (Hebrews 2:2).

Angels participated in the giving of the Law, and they also carried out the sentences of the Law.

ANGELS ENFORCE THE WORD

Look again Hebrews 2:2: "For if the word spoken through angels proved steadfast, and every transgression and disobedience received a just reward..." The word *transgression* means "to trespass, to go beyond the ordinary boundary"; indeed, "to break the rules." *Disobedience* means simply "to act against what has been commanded." Angels punish lawbreakers! This is why you must never assign angelic protection in your life if you are violating the law and disobeying authority. It is abundantly clear that angels respect, respond, and release the Word of God. As we have observed, the angels were present at the giving of the Law (Psalm 68:17), the Law came by angelic direction (Acts 7:53), the Law was "appointed through angels" (Galatians 3:19), and the Word was "spoken" in some cases by the angels (Hebrews 2:2). We conclude from these scriptures that obedience to the Word of God is vital to release angelic activity. Also, could it be possible that angels are grieved by humans who transgress God's laws? As we witnessed earlier, both angels and demons are arranged in military hierarchy; therefore, rebellion would be considered grievous. Could it be that angelic help is stifled by rebellious activity?

ANGELS AND THE CONFESSED WORD

Moving from the negative to the positive, we see that angels are activated and released when we confess, by faith, the Word of God: "Bless the LORD, you His angels, who excel in strength, who do His word, heeding the voice of His word. Bless the LORD, all you His hosts, you ministers of His, who do His pleasure" (Psalm 103:20–21). Here this scripture gives us clear direction on how angels are moved by God's Word. Notice that the Word is powerfully embraced by the hosts of heaven in an atmosphere of worship. When a believer worships, angels gather.

Obedience to the Word of God is vital to release angelic activity.

Secondly, angels "do His word." This is their vocation and purpose. Angels will cause the Word of God to come to pass in the lives of believers.

Third, notice that when the Word is voiced, angels are activated. When a faithful Christian says aloud the Word God has released in him or her, that Word is carried forth on the wings of angels to be answered. Angels do God's Word and respond to the Word spoken aloud! Angels cannot read your mind. When you confess the Word of God by faith out of your mouth, angels move instantly. It is their joy to speedily bring your confession to pass! As we obey, heed, and confess the Word of God, we bring our angelic allies into full partnership. They will bring to pass what God has promised.

Angels are activated and released when
we confess, by faith, the Word of God.

At a staff meeting in our church some years ago, there was a report of a financial need. I prayed and dispatched harvest angels to go get what God's Word had promised us. Before the meeting ended, a local businessman brought in a five-figure check that met the need. God's angels moved when the promise of God's Word was embraced and spoken.

Chapter Fourteen

ANSWER

PRAYER

"...the prayers of the saints, ascended before God from the angel's hands" (Revelation 8:4).

NGELIC ACTIVITY SWIRLS AROUND AND MINGLES WITH things of the Spirit. We have already observed how angels are connected to the glory of worship and to the needs of believers. Angels are especially attuned to the spiritual discipline of prayer. Angels are activated by a sincere heart seeking God in prayer. It appears in Scripture that angelic worship includes watching over the prayers of believers. On two occasions angels are viewed as attending the prayers of believers.

First, in the dramatic worship scene found in Revelation 5, the Lamb takes the scroll from the strong angel. This scroll recounts all of the trials of humanity across the ages. Only our Lord Jesus, by His sacrifice, can restore what has been lost. In this powerful vision, the Lamb bears the visible signs of having been slain. (See Revelation 5:6–7.)

When the Lion/Lamb seizes the scroll, triumphant worship breaks out among those redeemed and among the heavenly hosts. As the praise begins, there is a mysterious mention of angels and our prayers: "Now when He had taken the scroll, the four living creatures and the twenty-four elders fell down before the Lamb, each having a harp, and golden bowls full of incense, which are the prayers of the saints" (Revelation 5:8).

Angels of worship attend to the
sincere cries of God's people.

It appears the prayers of all believers across all time are being watched over by angels. Prayers are viewed as "golden bowls" of "incense." This image takes us back to temple worship where the incense burned before the cloud of glory, God's presence. Angels keep our prayers as a sweet smell before the throne of God. Prayers are cherished in heaven and are in the care of the worshiping hosts. In the Scripture reference above, the angel hosts play their harps (*kithara* in the Greek, from which we get the English word *guitar*). As they play and lead worship, the prayers ascend as incense before the throne of God: "And the smoke of the incense, with the prayers of the saints, ascended before God from the angel's hand. Then the angel took the censer, filled it with fire from the altar, and threw it to the earth. And there were noises, thunderings, lightnings, and an earthquake" (Revelation 8:4–5).

As this scene unfolds, the prayers of believers loose the seven trumpets of judgment on the earth. Notice our prayers "ascended before God from the angel's hand." Then our prayers are hurled back to the earth as fire! This powerful image of prayer is confirmed in Psalm 141:1–2: "LORD, I cry out to You; make haste to me! Give ear to my voice when I cry out to You. Let my prayer be set before You as incense, the lifting up of my hands as the evening sacrifice." Notice the image of incense and prayer. Angels of worship attend to the sincere cries of God's people.

NO PRAYER GOES UNNOTICED

Angels collect all of our prayers, and they are offered as a sacrifice to God. Until the answer is ready, they burn before the throne of God as a sweet sacrifice. Angels tend our prayers and are agents used to answer our prayers. In due season the Holy Spirit and the angels of fire move to answer the righteous prayers of believers. A clear example of how this works is recorded in Luke 1:8–12.

Zacharias was serving as the high priest and ministering by burning incense as all the people were in the outer court of the temple praying at the hour of incense. The people knew that prayer mixed with sacrifice and worship was powerful and effective. In that moment the invisible works of God became visible. Astonishingly, the angel of the Lord stood at the right side of the altar of incense. What was this angel doing? He was gathering the prayers of believers as he always did, but on that day he manifested himself to Zacharias. Why did the angel show himself? Because Zacharias and Elizabeth had been praying earnestly all their lives for a child. At the hour of incense, the hour of prayer, the angel who watches over prayer showed up. This scene ends with a fearful Zacharias doubting the word from Gabriel and being struck mute so he could not confess unbelief and contradict the word of faith claimed by his wife, Elizabeth. Angels respond to "the voice of His word" (Psalm 103:20); therefore, Gabriel would not allow a single word of unbelief to be voiced during Elizabeth's pregnancy.

A MOTHER'S ANSWERED PRAYER

My husband and oldest son work at the same place in Colusa, California. We live in Colusa, and our son lives thirty miles away. They work early hours. One morning after my husband left for work I could not sleep. I looked at the clock and it was 4:45 a.m. Our son was on my mind and heavy on my heart. I just thought I was being overprotective and tried to close my eyes to go back to sleep.

"There are angels among us. You never know if it's that person standing next to you in an elevator, behind you in line at the market, or even the pizza delivery guy!"

The weight got so heavy I could not lie down anymore. I called my husband at work and asked him if our son had gotten to work yet. He said no. By this time it was 5:20 a.m. and he was to start at 5:30. I started praying and asking God to please put His angels around my son and get him safely to work.

I was still praying for God's angels when, about twenty minutes later, I heard a car outside. As I opened the front door, my son was walking up to the door. His car was still running, driver's door open, and his head in his hands. He was crying, and he said, "Mom, I almost died."

He had fallen asleep at the wheel as he was crossing a two-mile bridge. As the road curved, his car went straight into the other lane and hit the cement wall. The car then lifted about one inch from the top of the wall. He woke up and struggled to back the car off the wall, scraping it for at least ten feet.

I hugged my son, and I told him what happened to me earlier and that I had prayed for God's angels to protect him. We both cried and thanked God for giving him a guardian angel.[1]

AN ANGEL TO THE RESCUE

There are angels among us. You never know if it's that person standing next to you in an elevator, behind you in line at the market, or even the pizza delivery guy!

One of my dearest friends worked as a full-time nanny for a very nice family of five that lived way out in the Indiana countryside. Being a mother-to-be herself, she certainly had her hands full with taking care of their children, and she did an amazing job!

I'd gone over there one weekend to spend some time with her and the kids while the parents were out of town. It was a wonderful December day and had started to get late. It was time for me to leave. It *really* snowed that day, so everything was completely covered. After I'd warmed my car, I was trying to back out and had somehow found myself no longer on their driveway but on their yard. That's when I got stuck. I tried rocking the car back and forth in my attempt to get the car out, but all that did was give them a pretty decent yard job! Feeling just awful about it, I went back inside and announced to my friend, "I'm stuck!" My friend was looking for shovels, salt, two by fours, anything that might help. "Surely these folks have tools; they live in the country!" No luck.

I'd gone back out to the car to have another go at it and was getting really frustrated. It was around 11:00 p.m. and very cold, and although the snowing has slowed to almost nothing coming down, it was difficult to get around since the snow from the day was so deep. Back in the car, I sat there thinking that I didn't want to worsen the near ditch I'd already dug into their front yard. I couldn't believe this. "How could I have done this?" I asked myself. I didn't even have anyone to call for help. I started to pray. After a few minutes, for some reason I glanced at my trip odometer. To my horror, it read the numbers 666. I became angry and yelled, "I rebuke this!" and quickly pushed the button, changing the odometer back to zero.

Just then, a small car with a Domino's Pizza delivery sign on top pulled up to the house. I thought, "Way out here? That's odd." A man got out of the car. With a big smile, he walked over and chuckled, "Looks like you could use a little help."

I was giddy with thankfulness and replied, "Oh, yes! Thank you! Thank you so much!"

He laughed and said that he'd give it a push while I gave it a little gas.

I sat in the car and looked behind me through the rear window. The man stood behind my car, and for a few moments, he looked at it in what appeared to be a very thoughtful way. It was like he was gathering information with his smiling eyes.

"I went to reach for my purse in the car to give him some cash for helping me out, and when I looked up, he'd already gone..."

"OK, then!" he called out. So I pressed gently on the gas pedal. I certainly didn't want to fling slush and mud on him.

He placed his hands on the trunk of my car and forward, up, and back onto the driveway I went. I thought, "Oh my! He didn't even lean!"

I got out of the car and was so surprised, all I could get out of my mouth was a barrage of thank yous and a "Wow, you're strong!"

He laughed and asked that I be very careful out there on the road.

I went to reach for my purse in the car to give him some cash for helping me out, and when I looked up, he'd already gone all the way back to where his car was on the road. He stood by his car and waved before getting in and pulling away.

I quickly jumped into my car and backed out to the road. He was gone. No taillights. No tire tracks in the snow.[2]

Your prayers matter to our Father and activate angelic assistance. No prayer goes unnoticed or unanswered.

WHAT DOES ALL THIS SAY TO US?

1. Angels abide in the secret place of prayer.

2. Angels are stirred and motivated by both individual and corporate prayer.

3. Prayer is best offered in a context of intense worship.

4. Angels watch over prayers yet to be answered.

5. Prayers are a pleasant and sweet aroma to God our Father.

6. Prayers rise to God from the hands of our angel allies.

7. Angels respond negatively to wrong words; negative confessions, curses, and unbelief hinder the miracle-working Word.

8. Prayers offered in passionate faith and trust in God will be answered by God and delivered by angels.

Your prayers matter to our Father and activate angelic assistance. Remember, no prayer goes unnoticed or unanswered. I realize to some of you that doesn't make sense, when you have prayed for healing and the healing hasn't come, or when you have suffered greatly and there seemed to be no relief. However, this passage shows us that our prayers have been entrusted to angels until their appointed time. As allies with the angels, we must be reassured by the power of prayer and spend time regularly with God.

Chapter Fifteen

MOVE *on*

MIRACLE GROUND

The point is this, when our King Jesus reigns as Lord,
the kingdom has come! Therefore, we are living in a
time of kingdom breakthrough.

ANGELIC ACTIVITY IS ON THE INCREASE IN THESE LAST
days. The reason for supernatural operations is twofold.
First, as we move toward the end, human options
begin to dwindle. Human ingenuity creates a world that rushes
toward ruin and chaos. As this time approaches, God releases
more angelic intervention to protect His people and to promote
His kingdom. Furthermore, for the past century, the church

has been experiencing the renewal and restoration of the Pentecostal gifts. Beginning at Azusa Street in the early twentieth century and continuing to this very day, a mighty outpouring of the Holy Spirit is sweeping across our world. Historians tell us that we are actually in the third wave of this worldwide move of the Spirit. Conversions to Christianity in the third world are reaching record numbers. Even the Islamic world is being powerfully impacted by the supernatural. Visions, dreams, and angels are appearing even where there is no missionary presence.

As churches and ministries embrace charismatic ministry, old divisions are falling away and kingdom unity is spreading worldwide. The last days' church must be kingdom oriented in order to release the supernatural, including miraculous angelic assistance.

KINGDOM MINISTRY

As we discuss the miracle ground that angels operate from, it is essential for us to know how to be in prime position to receive and activate their supernatural influence in our world. One of the main things to understand is how the kingdom of God works in relationship to us and the earth realm. As I have already pointed out, there are certain kingdom laws in the Word of God that angels abide by, and if we are to benefit from them as our allies, we need to abide by those laws as well. Our understanding of God's kingdom will help us understand the connection between the laws of the kingdom and our angelic allies.

According to Luke 17:21, the kingdom of God dwells within us. So if Jesus is Lord in our lives, then His kingdom has come through us. Yet we will only have full access to it and its resources once we are born again by the Spirit of God. (See John 3:5.) This access to kingdom resources requires a willingness to change (repent) and a submissive, broken spirit. (See Matthew 3:2; 6:33.) With the kingdom of God being present all around us through angelic miracles, old divisions between churches being broken down, and even conversions in the Islamic countries, it is clear that we are living in a time of kingdom breakthrough.

The last days' church must be kingdom oriented in order to release the supernatural, including miraculous angelic assistance.

But not only is the kingdom of God here now, it is also yet to come. Hebrews 2:8–9 says, "But now we do not yet see all things put under him. But we see Jesus." We do not yet see all of the aspects and inner workings of God's kingdom, but its fullness is yet to come because we are still waiting for Jesus to return to the earth a second time. In John 18:36 Jesus confirms this by saying that the kingdom of God is "not of this world."

The kingdom breaks through into the "now" by the Holy Spirit. In the letters of Paul, he calls the baptism of the Holy Spirit a guarantee of the powers of the world to come in the here and now! Furthermore, the powers of the kingdom are released at our sealing and anointing. (See 2 Corinthians 1:21–22; Ephesians 1:14.) I am convinced that many Christians are children of the kingdom but are not sons! All who are saved are children, yet the rights of sonship, which include angels, miracles, signs, and wonders, belong to those who have been baptized in the Holy Spirit.

The Holy Spirit releases the power of the kingdom now! Angels are a part of that realm we call "the kingdom of heaven." When a church or a believer is willing to sell out to all God has, the angelic activity will increase exponentially! In a hurting, sad, and dirty world, we need this kingdom that is "righteousness and peace and joy in the Holy Spirit" (Romans 14:17) to be activated.

Now that we have explored how we can be in position to receive and/or activate the kingdom of heaven with angelic ministry, let's look at some of the grounds upon which angels tread in order to impact the earth with kingdom power.

ANGELIC MINISTRY IN THE CHURCH

At Abba's House (Central Baptist Church, Chattanooga, TN), where I have served for thirty years, we have moved from a traditional ministry to what some call charismatic. The transition began in 1989 and continues until this day. Since 1993 angel sightings, angelic singing, orbs of light, and bursts of fire have taken place. All of these manifestations occurred after I was baptized in the Holy Spirit and as the church moved into that realm. It is my belief that angelic ministry in today's kingdom church is similar to what took place in the New Testament church.

All who are saved are children,
yet the rights of sonship, which
include angels, miracles, signs, and
wonders, belong to those who have
been baptized in the Holy Spirit.

When we read the New Testament, we find its pages filled with angelic activity. When the church brings those who are lost to a saving knowledge of Jesus Christ, the angels join in the celebration and praise for their conversion. Scripture says that when the lost are found, "there is joy in the presence of the angels" (Luke 15:10). When the church gathers for worship, angels gather with us (Hebrews 12:22). Angels exhibit a strong curiosity about believers' spiritual lives (1 Peter 1:12). Undoubtedly because of their large number, their activity in the spiritual realm, and their presence among the members of the kingdom church, we are warned not to make the angels objects of our worship (Colossians 2:18). (See addendum for more information on this.)

In his book *The Truth About Angels*, Terry Law illustrates how angels are moved by our worship. He shares several stories that tell of angelic activity in churches.[1]

> Sharon Abrams, a physician's wife who attends Agape Church, told of seeing two angels during a church service. The angels were hovering over the congregation with their arms outstretched. They were light-skinned and had light-colored hair, and they stood seven or eight feet tall. Abrams wrote: "Their faces were broad with high cheekbones and beautiful smiles. They looked like men except they did not have beards. There was an innocence to their faces, and the joy of their expressions was wonderful. They did not wear shoes, but wore long white gowns with gold braid. I cannot remember exactly where the braid was located on the gowns. I knew they were in the service because of our praise and worship...because Jesus was being lifted up and adored. I sensed there were many more beings

present in the auditorium, but I was only able to see those two."[2]

Marilyn Cappo of Louisville Covenant Church in Kentucky says she has seen angels on a number of occasions. She reported seeing three angels dancing on the roof of a house where a home group was meeting. One of them was playing something like a small harp, perhaps a lyre. Later, during a church morning worship service, she saw a nine-foot angel standing behind the worship leader. Most recently, she said she has seen two angels standing on the front platform of her church during several different services. She described them this way:

"They are a little over six feet tall and dressed in white. They do not speak but raise their wings when songs are sung of direct praise to the Father.

"They stand to the left of the pulpit, watching the congregation, and look at us expectantly. I have seen them off and on over a period of months and have prayed often to understand their purpose and mission at our church. One morning one of them walked over behind the pastor and spread his wings as our pastor was making declarative statements about God to us. The angels appear to be waiting for us to do something and always watch intently."

Patsy Burton of Wethersfield, Essex, in England, wrote of hearing angels singing during a church service. She said the "clarity, pitch and harmony was absolutely incredible. In fact, there are no words to describe how they sounded."

In *Somewhere Angels*, one of the best books that I have found on angels, author Larry Libby wrote about a worship meeting in Alaska: "Outside, the winter wind moaned and hissed against the frosted church windows. But inside the little church, people were warm and happy and singing song after song of praise to God...something mysterious and wonderful happened that icy, starlit night. After one last praise song...people stopped singing. The musicians put down their instruments. But somehow, the singing kept going. Everyone heard it. The beautiful praise music kept rolling on and on for a little while, like a long, silvery echo."[3]

---

*When a believer refuses to submit
to apostles, prophets, evangelists,
pastors, and teachers, then the angels
that accompany them are insulted
and will not release blessing.*

ANGELS AND KINGDOM LEADERSHIP

Furthermore, angels accompany those who serve in the fivefold ministry. Let's look carefully at this often-quoted but misunderstood scripture on angels: "Do not forget to entertain strangers, for by so doing some have unwittingly entertained angels" (Hebrews 13:2).

This verse, when viewed in context, concerns church authority and order. Believers are called to "remember those who rule over you, who have spoken the word of God to you" (Hebrews 13:7). Note again the following mandate: "Obey those who rule over you, and be submissive, for they watch out for your souls.... Let them do so with joy and not with grief, for that would be unprofitable for you" (Hebrews 13:17). The point is quite clear: angels accompany those who lead, speak the Word of God, teach faith, and watch for your souls, and they release profit or prosperity. When a believer refuses to submit to apostles, prophets, evangelists, pastors, and teachers, then the angels that accompany them are insulted and will not release blessing. Those who mock and make fun of men and women of God are blocking the ministry of angels.

> *Only as we receive those whom God*
> *sets over us can we have the full*
> *ministry of the hosts at their disposal.*

Let's take a look at a couple stories that illustrate God's care for His chosen leaders through the intervention of angels. The first story tells how a whole mission headquarters was kept from certain calamity because a man of God was there to serve.

> The Reverend John G. Paton, pioneer missionary in the New Hebrides Islands, told a thrilling story involving the protective care of angels. Hostile natives surrounded his mission headquarters one night, intent on burning the Patons out and killing them. John Paton and his wife prayed all during that terror-filled night that God would deliver them. When daylight came they were amazed to see that, unaccountably, the attackers had left. They thanked God for delivering them.

A year later, the chief of the tribe was converted to Jesus Christ, and Mr. Paton, remembering what had happened, asked the chief what had kept him and his men from burning down the house and killing them. The chief replied in surprise, "Who were all those men you had with you there?" The missionary answered, "There were no men there; just my wife and I." The chief argued that they had seen many men standing guard—hundreds of big men in shining garments with drawn swords in their hands. They seemed to circle the mission station so that the natives were afraid to attack. Only then did Mr. Paton realize that God had sent His angels to protect them. The chief agreed that there was no other explanation.[4]

A missionary who came home for a short break shared this story at his home church in Michigan:

While serving at a small field hospital in Africa, every two weeks I traveled by bicycle through the jungle to a nearby city for supplies. This was a journey of two days and required camping overnight at the halfway point. On one of these journeys, I arrived in the city where I planned to collect money from a bank, purchase medicine and supplies, and then begin my two-day journey back to the field hospital.

Upon arrival in the city, I observed two men fighting, one of whom had been seriously injured. I treated him for his injuries and at the same time talked to him about the Lord. I then traveled two days, camping overnight, and arrived home without incident.

Two weeks later I repeated my journey. Upon arriving in the city, I was approached by the young man I had treated. He told me that he had known I carried money and medicines. He said, "Some friends and I followed you into the jungle, knowing you would camp overnight. We planned to kill you and take your money and the drugs. But just as we were about to move into your camp, we saw that twenty-six armed guards surrounded you." At this, I laughed and said that I was certainly all alone in that jungle campsite.

The young man pressed the point, however, and said, "No, sir, I was not the only person to see the guards; my friends also saw them and we all counted them. It was because of those guards that we were afraid and left you alone."

At this point in the sermon, one of the men in the congregation jumped to his feet and interrupted the missionary and asked if he could tell him the exact day this happened. The missionary told the congregation the date, and the man who interrupted told him this story.

"On the night of your incident in Africa, it was morning here and I was preparing to go play golf. I was about to putt when I felt the urge to pray for you. In fact, the urging of the Lord was so strong; I called some men in this church to meet with me here in the sanctuary to pray for you. Would all of those men who met with me on that day stand up?"

The men who had met together to pray that day stood up. The missionary wasn't concerned with who they were; he was too busy counting how many men he saw. There were twenty-six men.[5]

These stories make it clear that when we welcome the ministries of godly men and women, we entertain the angels who are assigned to them. Those accompanying angels are released in the community being visited by the guest; there they battle the ruling powers of the enemy and release the miracles of God. Only as we receive those whom God sets over us can we have the full ministry of the hosts at their disposal.

As faith increases and the church operates in kingdom power, our angelic allies will help us take dominion in our communities and our nations.

Even the business community can turn from loss to profit by welcoming God's servants and their angelic helpers. In the election of 2008, it is interesting that the financial downturn and loss of profit in America happened when the media and the Left mocked the faith of Sarah Palin. *Newsweek* mocked her charismatic expressions, and the media laughed. Angels of profit were insulted as this woman of God was not respected. You can mark the loss of profit in the stock market from the mocking of her charismatic faith. Angels were insulted and businesses failed. (See Hebrews 13:2, 17.)

ANGELS AND AWAKENING

The hosts of heaven can move on behalf of our Western nations again only if we respect the spiritual leaders God sends. When this happens, angels will come with fire to cleanse and to rekindle our spiritual lives. This will result in a release of super-natural power and resources. Hebrews 1:7 declares that angels are flames of fire. Pentecostal fire includes angelic fire released to do its powerful work in the earth. (Even our speaking in tongues is called by the Scriptures "tongues of angels," as we see in 1 Corinthians 13:1.) As faith increases and the church operates in kingdom power, our angelic allies will help us take dominion in our communities and our nations. Let us activate our angels by making the kingdom of God our priority. God will order the angels into our dimension as we move in the power of the Holy Spirit.

Section Four

WHEN

ANGELS

VINDICATE

Chapter Sixteen

EXECUTE
GOD'S WRATH

God has already announced the victory and set His
war plan in writing in Scripture, especially in the
Book of Revelation. When you turn the pages in Revelation, angelic activity is on every page.

A NGELIC ACTIVITY ERUPTS AT THE MIGHTY EPOCHS OF
God's kingdom. As we have observed, angels sang and
shouted as God called the creation out of nothing.
Angels conveyed the glory of God with a backslidden Judah
to Babylonian captivity. Angels covered God's ancient people
during their captivity. Angels welcomed the Messiah above

Bethlehem fields with a sound and light show not seen since Creation. Sadly, the same angels who raised the curtain on our planet and have guarded its destiny will also release the judgments that are yet to come.

GOD'S WRATH FULLY RELEASED

The last book in the Bible records two phenomena intensifying at the same time. Worship intensifies in a powerful crescendo that shakes all of creation. Conversely, wars and catastrophes intensify. God will judge every failed human system and then every human being outside of Christ. Angelic activity in judging nations and in times of war is evident in Scripture and history. In 1 Chronicles 21, one angel stretched his sword over Jerusalem, and 70,000 men of Israel died in a plague. Angels announced the judgment of Sodom and Gomorrah in Genesis 19. In 2 Kings 19, Hezekiah prayed, and one warring angel killed 185,000 Assyrians, thwarting their occupation of Israel. In Acts 12, an angel struck down King Herod because of his pride. Only in the next life will we understand how many dictators, presidents, kings, sheikhs, and prime ministers have had their careers affected by angels. Furthermore, we will know then how many battles were won or lost at the hand of the angel allies. Perhaps then we will understand the angelic involvement that has swayed the nations.

Angels will bring down false religions, and it is angels who judge the great religious harlot.

All of these judgments pale in comparison to the End Time scenario of Revelation. Angels are the enforcers of God's wrath on the cursed earth. When we turn the pages of Revelation, there is an explosion of angelic activity like never before witnessed on Planet Earth. In the opening three chapters, angels are assigned to the church and are active in communicating God's will. In Revelation chapters 4 and 5 angels join all of creation in the most majestic worship service ever assembled.

After that phenomenal worship, angels begin to blow trumpets that summon horrific judgments on the planet. As we continue to read in Revelation 6, we see the horror of wars, famines, plagues, and natural disasters claim one-third of the human population of earth. Interestingly, at the sixth trumpet, angels of judgment bound in the river Euphrates are released to kill that one-third of humanity mentioned earlier. Yes, from Iraq, ancient Babylon will issue horrific bloodshed on Earth.

As we continue to turn the pages of Revelation we see an extreme intensification occur. Chapters 15 through 16 of Revelation record the pouring out of seven bowls of wrath on the earth. Images such as the river of blood brought on by angelic actions are terrifying. Angels will bring down false religions, and it is angels who judge the great religious harlot in Revelation 17:1–2: "Then one of the seven angels who had the seven bowls came and talked with me, saying to me, 'Come, I will show you the judgment of the great harlot who sits on many waters, with whom the kings of the earth committed fornication, and the inhabitants of the earth were made drunk with the wine of her fornication.'"

Angels announce the collapse of Wall Street and all other world markets. The fear that gripped our nation in these current seasons of recession and depression is nothing in comparison to that final hour.

> After these things I saw another angel coming down from heaven, having great authority, and the earth was illuminated with his glory. And he cried mightily with a loud voice, saying, "Babylon the great is fallen, is fallen, and has become a dwelling place of demons, a prison for every foul spirit, and a cage for every unclean and hated bird! For all the nations have drunk of the wine of the wrath of her fornication, the kings of the earth have committed fornication with her, and the merchants of the earth have become rich through the abundance of her luxury." And I heard another voice from heaven saying, "Come out of her, my people, lest you share in her sins, and lest you receive of her plagues."
> —REVELATION 18:1–4

All of the greed, thievery, and luxury will be brought down by the angels of God.

Let the idea that angels are small effervescent creatures fluttering around leave you forever. Angels are mighty warriors and, in the last days, will execute God's wrath without mercy!

On the final pages of Revelation, angels accompany our Lord Jesus at His Second Coming. The mighty hosts of heaven who are His palace guards come to "mop up" the remaining foes on Earth. Paul describes that scene vividly: "And to give you who are troubled rest with us when the Lord Jesus is revealed from heaven with His mighty angels, in flaming fire taking vengeance on those who do not know God, and on those who do not obey the gospel of our Lord Jesus Christ" (2 Thessalonians 1:7–8). The Lord will come with mighty angels to finish off the enemy. Angels will implement the death of the wicked.

God will avenge His people at the revelation of Jesus Christ. Our Lord will be revealed with His "mighty angels." The word *mighty* translates *dunamis*, which means "explosive power." These angels will come in *phlox pur*, or "flaming fire," to purify the universe and punish the wicked! Second Thessalonians 1:9 says this punishment will be "everlasting destruction from the presence of the Lord."

Then Satan will be captured and contained by one mighty angel.

> Then I saw an angel coming down from heaven, having the key to the bottomless pit and a great chain in his hand. He laid hold of the dragon, that serpent of old, who is the Devil and Satan, and bound him for a thousand years; and he cast him into the bottomless pit, and shut him up, and set a seal on him, so that he should deceive the nations no more till the thousand years were finished. But after these things he must be released for a little while.
>
> …The devil, who deceived them, was cast into the lake of fire and brimstone where the beast and the false prophet are. And they will be tormented day and night forever and ever.
>
> —REVELATION 20:1–3, 10

All of the unsaved will be cast into hell by angels! Let the idea that angels are small effervescent creatures fluttering around leave you forever. Angels are mighty warriors and, in the last days, will execute God's wrath without mercy!

Finally, angels will announce the rapture of the church. Our glorious translation will remove the final restraint, and God will unleash the final judgment: "For the Lord Himself will descend from heaven with a shout, with the voice of an archangel, and with the trumpet of God. And the dead in Christ will rise first" (1 Thessalonians 4:16).

ANGELS SING A SONG OF END TIMES DISASTERS

Further proof of angelic activity in the last days is a story a missionary to China tells about angels warning of End Times disaster through rural Chinese churchgoers who were singing in the Spirit during a 1995 worship service. The account reads as follows:

> The whole province of Shandong, in eastern China (population: 57 million), is in the midst of a sweeping revival. For fear of arrest, believers meet secretly in house churches, often by candlelight. At a 1995 meeting in Shandong, everyone was singing "in the Spirit" together (1 Corinthians 14:15), not in their own language, but "as the Spirit gave them utterance," all in harmony but all singing different words.
>
> Someone audiotaped the meeting. Later, when they played back the cassette, they were shocked! What they heard was not what had happened there at all—but the sound of angels singing in

Mandarin—a song they had never heard before, and with a musical accompaniment that had not been there!!! When my friend first heard the tape, before anyone told him what it was, he exclaimed, "Those are angels!!" Actually, there was no other explanation. A Chinese Christian co-worker translated the tape. Below are the actual words sung by the angels! Note that the words express ideas with which these rural Chinese peasants were not familiar.

The End Is Near: Rescue Souls

The famine is becoming more and more critical. There are more and more earthquakes. The situation is becoming more and more sinister. People are fighting against each other, nation against nation. Disasters are more and more severe.

The whole environment is deteriorating. Disasters are more and more severe. People's hearts are wicked, and they do not worship the true God. Disasters are more and more severe.

Floods and droughts are more and more frequent. There is more and more homosexuality and incurable diseases. Disasters are more and more severe.

The climates are becoming more and more abnormal. The earth is more and more restless. The skies have been broken. The atmosphere is distorted. Disasters are more and more severe.

Chorus

The end is near. The revelation of love
has been manifested. Rise up, rise up, rescue souls. The end is near. Rise up, rise up,
rescue souls.[1]

GOD'S WRATH ON SATAN RELEASED AT THE CROSS

While I have shown through Scripture and real-life events that
wars and catastrophes increase toward the close of time, let me
make it clear that all demonic spirits are already defeated. At the
cross and empty tomb, Christ won a transdimensional, cosmic
victory over all the forces of darkness. The Bible affirms this
truth. At Jesus's ascension, He laid claim to full authority in
heaven and earth: "And Jesus came and spoke to them, saying,
'All authority has been given to Me in heaven and on earth'"
(Matthew 28:18).

In a cosmic display of power, Jesus stripped the forces of
darkness of their rights and authority: "... having wiped out
the handwriting of requirements that was against us, which was
contrary to us. And He has taken it out of the way, having nailed
it to the cross. Having disarmed principalities and powers, He
made a public spectacle of them, triumphing over them in it"
(Colossians 2:14–15).

He destroyed the devil's threat of death and his right to
hold captive those who come to Christ: "Inasmuch then as the
children have partaken of flesh and blood, He Himself likewise shared in the same, that through death He might destroy
him who had the power of death, that is, the devil, and release
those who through fear of death were all their lifetime subject to
bondage" (Hebrews 2:14–15).

All of the forces of darkness are subject to Jesus. As we have seen, Jesus has defeated them all in the eternal realms; we are here to enforce the victory already won. "...who has gone into heaven and is at the right hand of God, angels and authorities and powers having been made subject to Him" (1 Peter 3:22).

The enemy is subject to Jesus but not subject to those who are not Christ's followers.

Though the war is won, we must enforce the victory of Christ. One of the reasons the enemy is here is to train followers for the future world. More significantly, the enemy is here for you to defeat him and display God's wisdom in saving you. (See chapter 6.)

> *We have the privilege to fight*
> *alongside our angel allies who*
> *enforce the victory already won!*

History has an example that might help you understand this concept. The War of 1812 was over, and peace agreements had been reached when the Battle of New Orleans was fought. Andrew Jackson led the army to a great victory in New Orleans; however, one of the greatest battles of that century served no purpose beyond that of making Andrew Jackson president.

Likewise, our victory was won by Jesus Christ at the cross and the empty tomb. Yet, like the War of 1812 and the Battle of New Orleans, we are still in a battle, even though the war has been won. However, in this battle, we have the privilege to fight alongside our angel allies who enforce the victory already won!

The war is won, but we are in the final countdown to its finish. The Scriptures are very clear on the angelic actions at the end of the age, especially in the Book of Revelation where angelic activity is recorded on almost every page. We can be confident in our God who has already announced the victory and set His war plan in writing in Scripture.

Chapter Seventeen

ESCORT

BELIEVERS HOME

O come, angel band, / Come and around me stand; /
O bear me away on your snowy wings / To my eternal
home.

As we come to the close of this book, let us trace the ministry of angels throughout the life of a believer until the moment of death. In order to make sense of angelic behavior, we must remember that they are very curious about humanity. They have their eyes on you! Angels are curious creatures when it comes to mankind and the things of salvation.

Angels and
The Very Young

Throughout your life, there are watching angels just a thought away. When you were born, an angel was assigned to be with you: "Take heed that you do not despise one of these little ones, for I say to you that in heaven their angels always see the face of My Father who is in heaven" (Matthew 18:10).

Angels access the Father face-to-face on behalf of the little ones. These angels are not called guardian angels. Angels do watch over believers, but the idea that angels function to guard little children is not biblical and does not square with the abuse and death of little children around us. Angels do convey the souls of children who are underage to glory.

> When the Alfred P. Murrah Building was bombed on April 19, 1995, it was a tragedy beyond belief. Yet Bill and Kathryn Brunk mourned the deaths, especially the death of so many children in the day-care center.
>
> Then, one night as they were talking, Bill suddenly stopped mid-sentence and closed his eyes as an astonishing vision took place. After what seemed like several minutes, he opened his eyes and tried to speak but at first was unable to find words.
>
> Finally he said, "Kathryn, I just saw the Murrah Building. It was right after the bomb exploded. There were angels everywhere, and they were tenderly caring for the victims. Many of the angels were already paired up with those for whom they had come and were headed to heaven. It was so beautiful. Kathryn, I know if you could paint what

I just saw, it would help those who have lost loved ones." Still pondering his words, the next day Kathryn ran into an old friend that she hadn't seen in four years. Anita, a quiet, conservative, business-woman, had an air of excitement about her that day. Kathryn was amazed to learn that over a three-day period Anita had seen hundreds of angels covering the Murrah Building in a series of visions.

"The largest concentration of angels was in the lower corner [where the children's day care had been]," explained Anita. "But they were also flying throughout the honeycomb of offices. Many angels were still arriving, but some had already collected their beloved ones and were going home. Heaven was at the top and grew brighter and brighter the higher they flew. It was so beautiful!"

Anita continued, "The following day the vision came again, but this time there were fewer angels—perhaps 50 or 60. On the third day the vision returned, but only about 6 angels remained."

"I know these visions were given to me for a purpose," said Anita. "As I prayed, you came to mind. I was afraid my memory would lose the vision's intensity, and I didn't want to omit a single detail."

Anita's descriptions to Kathryn detailed specific areas of the building and how the angels were carrying precious loved ones to heaven. To confirm what Anita saw, Kathryn told her about Bill's vision. Neither Anita nor Bill had ever experienced God working in this way before.

Excited and awestruck, Kathryn began to sketch the scene. Later in her studio Kathryn painted the visions.

"Throughout this project I remained intensely prayerful, inviting God to guide my work," says Kathryn. "God went to great lengths to provide us with a visible image of His tremendous love and care. I feel grateful to have been allowed simply to hold the brushes."

Seeking to relay the tenderness and glory of God's heavenly messengers, Kathryn used an inventive method of overlaying reflective paint over the oils. This allows angelic activity to be seen when bright light is held close to the canvas. "To see into the spiritual realm," says Kathryn, "we have to be bearers of light."

Kathryn's two large canvases have been shown at a variety of gatherings. One depicts a fireman holding baby Baylee and depicts the child's first glimpse of God. The other painting is called *Beauty for Ashes*.[1]

Angels care for the eternal soul of a child before he or she reaches the age of accountability, a term used to describe the age when a child can make a responsible choice about a personal relationship with God. Jesus speaks of this angelic care in Matthew 18:10: "Take heed that you do not despise one of these little ones, for I say to you that in heaven their angels always see the face of My Father who is in heaven."

These visions, as seen by Bill and Kathryn Brunk and by Anita square with Scripture. We see in the New Testament Gospel of Luke that angels actually convey the souls of those who have died to heaven. "So it was that the beggar died, and was carried by the angels to Abraham's bosom" (Luke 16:22). Angels are assigned to see that children get to glory.

ANGELS AT THE TIME OF CONVERSION

Angels are watching when you come to Christ. In the heavenly dimension they see you weep your way to Jesus, trusting only in His precious blood and life-giving resurrection. Angels erupt in praise each time someone comes to faith in Jesus. Luke 15:10 says, "Likewise, I say to you, there is joy in the presence of the angels of God over one sinner who repents." Your angels lead the great company of angels in dancing, singing, and shouting over your new birth. Angels look in wonder upon your life as you grow and are changed by the gospel: "To them it was revealed that, not to themselves, but to us they were ministering the things which now have been reported to you through those who have preached the gospel to you by the Holy Spirit sent from heaven—things which angels desire to look into" (1 Peter 1:12). Isn't that wonderful?

Angels care for the eternal soul of a child before he or she reaches the age of accountability.

Charlie Carty tells how angels played a significant part in his conversion experience:

[One Sunday] my wife was to be baptized in our local church where we had been attending. I had never been baptized and was hesitant about doing so. The day we arrived at the church, when she was going to make her profession of faith and accept the Lord, I drove to the church but had made up my mind that I was not ready yet. When we arrived at the church, I let her out at the door and was parking the van when I felt someone with me.

I felt a hand around my shoulder, and in my head I heard my guardian angel's voice saying, "Charlie, it's time to make a commitment. Trust me and lean on me, and I will be there with you always."

I realized this was a voice I had heard before, in Vietnam, on my motorcycle, and outside a business in the dark. I was still confused and went into the church for service. When the call was given, my wife went forward to profess her faith, and as I sat there, I felt a pressure on my shoulder and I found myself getting up and going forward. I knelt at the prayer bench beside my wife and accepted Jesus as my Savior.[2]

Charlie goes on in his story to share more about his angelic encounters, but one thing is evident: his angel stayed with him throughout his life to see God's plans and purposes fulfilled that day when Charlie accepted the Lord into his life. What a party there must have been in heaven that Sunday morning with both Charlie and his wife giving their lives to Jesus!

*Angels erupt in praise each time
someone comes to faith in Jesus.*

ANGELS WITH US
ON LIFE'S JOURNEY

The angels leave the heavenly dimension and cross over to do for you everything that is needed along life's journey. As you have seen in this book, angels direct, protect, strengthen, encourage, and bring favor, health, and provision. You cannot comprehend what we call "near misses," those times when an angel's hand moved you at just the right moment. You will never know how many times you received counsel and help from what you thought were strangers who were actually angels. "Let brotherly love continue. Do not forget to entertain strangers, for by so doing some have unwittingly entertained angels" (Hebrews 13:1–2).

Here is an angelic testimony that took place in Tennessee.

It happened just past midnight on March 26, 1993, to Vincent Tan, an analytical chemist who works in Chattanooga. Weeks were spent tracing this incident and have confirmed it with two reputable Christian leaders, his pastor and, finally, even Vincent himself. The following is a precisely recorded account:

Vincent was born Tan Ban Soon in Singapore of Chinese Buddhist parents. A few years ago as a young boy in Singapore, he was in the library reading a book on nuclear physics and discovered an offer for a Bible course stuck between some pages. He ordered the course and later became a Christian. He came to the U.S. to attend a Christian college, then gave himself the Western name of Vincent. After four years, he graduated with a major in science. He has been very active in his church and in sharing his faith.

On the night of Thursday, March 25, 1993, Vincent was working late in his laboratory to complete tests due on Friday. During the evening he moved his car close to the front door of the building, since there had recently been criminal activity in the area. From time to time he looked out the window into the almost empty parking lot to check on his car. At 1:30 a.m. he finished working in his lab. As he was preparing to lock the door, he saw a person standing by the passenger side of his car. Vincent assumed the man was trying to steal his car. He noted that the stranger was of medium build with clean-cut, straight hair and had on a T-shirt, blue jeans, and white tennis shoes. Unsure what to do, he went back into the lab and prayed, "Lord, help me to do what I have to do. Do I have to use chi-sao?" Chi-sao (pronounced "chee'-sow-o") is a form of martial art in which Vincent is proficient.

To be extra safe, he looked around the lab and picked up an 18-inch metal rod, held it behind him, and stuck his head out the door. He said, "Hi, can I help you?"

The stranger answered, "Hi, Vincent."

Startled, Vincent asked, "Do I know you?"

The stranger replied, "Not really."

"What is your name? Who are you?" Vincent probed.

The stranger said, "I have the name of your primary and secondary school." He added, "I'm a friend. You don't have to use chi-sao or the rod on me."

His voice had unusual authority, and it seemed he knew the question before it was asked. Now Vincent was really startled. No one, not even his best friend in this country, was familiar with chi-sao, nor did anyone even know that he knew it. Also, there was no way the stranger could have seen the rod behind his back.

Vincent later reflected that the stranger had used terminology ("primary and secondary school") of Singapore and not the U.S., and that name of his school back in Singapore was St. Gabriel. The stranger was saying that his name was Gabriel!

"How do you know that?" Vincent asked.

"I know," the stranger replied. "By the way, Mum is fine."

Vincent was startled again. Just the week before, his sister had called from Singapore saying that his mother had heart complications, and Vincent had been quite worried about her.

Gabriel continued, "You love the Lord very much, don't you?"

"That's right," Vincent replied.

"He loves you very much too," Gabriel said. Then he added, "He is coming very, very soon." He seemed to emphasize the "very soon."

Vincent answered, "That's great!"

Gabriel then asked, "Can I have a cup of water?"

Vincent said, "Sure," and turned momentarily to get him the water. Then he decided to invite the stranger inside to drink from the water fountain. He turned back to invite him inside—but Gabriel was not there. He had suddenly and inexplicably vanished! Vincent had not turned his head for more than three seconds.

There was no place for the stranger to have gone. Puzzled, and not wanting to go back into the lab, Vincent laid the metal rod down by the front door and headed to his home outside of Chattanooga. When he came back to work later that morning, he wondered if he had dreamed the whole experience. As a scientist, he wanted to prove whether it had really happened. When he got to the building, he found the metal rod lying by the door just where he had left it. He knew he had not been dreaming. Upon entering the lab, the first thing he did was to lock himself in the restroom and kneel in prayer. "Show me what to do, Lord. I know what I remember. If I'm supposed to share it, I must believe it myself," Vincent pleaded. He then sat down at his computer and recorded every word said and everything that had happened.

That night, March 26, 1993, in a dream Vincent relived the whole experience, seeing himself and word for word hearing the whole conversation. He awoke at about 3:30 a.m. and wrote down every word in the dream and the description of the stranger. What he wrote from the dream confirmed every detail he had written earlier. Also, a week after the experience, he learned that his mother had received needed surgery and was recuperating nicely—and that the medical decision about her improved condition came a week earlier at about the very same hour as he was talking with Gabriel!

On July 29, 1993, Vincent was asked what effect this experience has had on him. He said he believes more strongly now that we should be ready every day for the Lord's coming, and not worry about which day He will come. He said the experience has intensified his dedication, causing him to spend more devotional time than before, wanting to know more about God and be closer to Him. For some time, even before that experience, Vincent said he had been asking God, "Am I ready, right now?" Now, more meaningfully than ever, this writer is asking that same question.[3]

Angels watch over you as you fulfill your life's purposes, and your achievements are a spectacular vision for angels. Make no mistake; your life is on display at all times. You may hide the unrighteous actions of your life from men, but every moment is seen by God and the angels.

> I charge you before God and the Lord Jesus Christ
> and the elect angels that you observe these things
> without prejudice, doing nothing with partiality.
> Do not lay hands on anyone hastily, nor share in
> other people's sins; keep yourself pure.
> —1 TIMOTHY 5:21–22

The holy angels see our actions, and God sees the intent of our hearts; He warns us to keep ourselves not only from sin but also from prejudice and flippant attitudes toward others.

*You will never know how many times
you received counsel and help from
what you thought were strangers
who were actually angels.*

Our solemn responsibilities before God are also observed by angels. It is likely that angels are unusual agents of chastening and correction when we fail to obey heaven's charge to us.

> And without controversy great is the mystery of godliness: God was manifested in the flesh, justified in the Spirit, seen by angels, preached among the Gentiles, believed on in the world, received up in glory.
>
> —1 Timothy 3:16

Angels are a part of the wonder, mystery, and majesty of the Christian experience.

ANGELS AND SPIRIT-BAPTIZED BELIEVERS

Angelic ministry operates in the lives of all believers. Those who embrace the baptism of the Holy Spirit can have a deeper involvement with angels. The gift of the Holy Spirit is clearly a down payment of the heavenly life to come. Ephesians 1:14 says that it is "the guarantee of our inheritance until the redemption of the purchased possession, to the praise of His glory." Therefore, there are certain common elements between angels and people of the Spirit.

One evidence of being filled with the Spirit is speaking in tongues. Speaking in tongues is something we share in common with the angels. Clearly Paul describes the ecstatic prayer experience as "tongues of angels." There are languages spoken by angels and given to believers by the Spirit for intercession, worship, and strengthening. Tongues edify and strengthen the believer: "Though I speak with the tongues of men and of angels, but have not love, I have become sounding brass or a clanging cymbal" (1 Corinthians 13:1). Notice the word *tongues* is plural, which means that there are a variety of dialects in this special gift. Perhaps the "tongues of fire" seen above the heads of the apostles on the Day of Pentecost were angelic manifestations. (See Acts 2:1–4.)

> And of the angels He says: "Who makes His angels spirits and His ministers a flame of fire."
> —HEBREWS 1:7

We must remember, as well, that demons are fallen angels who have the same language capacities. Therefore, counterfeits must be exposed and avoided: "…for those who were once enlightened, and have tasted the heavenly gift, and have become partakers of the Holy Spirit…" (Hebrews 6:4).

We can speak with the tongues of angels and can enjoy their heavenly provision. What is angel's food? We are not talking about a light, fluffy, white cake, although some might describe it as heavenly. Manna that fell from the skies and fed the children of Israel in the wilderness was angel's food! Psalm 78:24–25 says, "…had rained down manna on them to eat, and given them of the bread of heaven. Men ate angels' food; He sent them food to the full." Angels clearly provided this food. Angels will help sustain us as believers on our journey through life's difficulties.

Manna may not fall from the sky, but miraculous provision is common for those who walk in the power of the Holy Spirit.

The gift of the Holy Spirit is clearly a down payment of the heavenly life to come.

ANGELS AT LIFE'S END

In Luke 16:20–22 we see proof that angels gather around the deathbeds of believers. When the beggar Lazarus died, angels carried him to the other side: "So it was that the beggar died, and was carried by the angels to Abraham's bosom" (verse 22).

In another instance, Mrs. Margaret Lackey shared with me the account of her father's passing.

> It was difficult to watch Parkinson's take its toll on Papa, the name given to our dad when his first grandchild arrived. He had always been a vibrant, well-poised, well-dressed "Dapper Dan." As we and our brother Doyle made trips back home to help care for him, we watched his health decline. As tremors crept upon him we'd ask, "Why must someone who has so much to give have to suffer this way?"
>
> Mother, in poor health as well, having a pacemaker, congestive heart failure, and three stints in her heart, put her own health on hold to make sure Dad received the care he needed.
>
> For fifty-nine years he served as a full-time pastor and evangelist spreading the good news of

Jesus Christ. His messages brought hope, assuring those who listened that "the way of the cross leads home." He fought the Parkinson's battle for eleven years. Yet he never expressed anger or bitterness. When others complained for him, he would often say, "Jesus suffered for me."

On Sunday, June 11, 2006, our worst fears were realized. Mother called to tell us Dad's swallowing was completely gone and they were going to the hospital. He had chosen to have no feeding tube, no IVs—nothing to keep him here when this time came. When they arrived at the hospital, he told his physician he was tired and ready to go to his heavenly home. And to his family, he simply asked, "Please, let me go now."

For eight days family members and friends gathered around Papa's bed. One by one we talked to him, shared special memories, sang his favorite songs, read his favorite scriptures, and prayed. We thanked him for being an awesome dad and grandpa, a loving husband of sixty-one years, a dear brother, special friend, good neighbor, and wonderful mentor/pastor...

During those final hours, Dad would look at the ceiling in the right-hand corner of the room and with a smile no pain could hide, he'd speak to and wave to those he saw—friends and loved ones already on the other side. At one point he told Mother that Jesus was standing at the foot of his bed. Once I crept into his room in the wee morning hours, stood by his bed praying softly, thanking God for him and his life. I told him I loved him. He squeezed my hand, then he lifted his head, looked up, and waved as though he saw someone dear to him that he had not seen for a while. Curious about his sudden excitement, I asked, "Dad, who is it?"

"It's angels!" he said.

I didn't see them, but I felt their presence in the room, an awesome presence that filled the room and filled my heart—a moment I will treasure forever.

At 6:00 p.m. on Monday, June 19, family, friends, pastors, nurses, and hospice "angels" gathered in Dad's room, surrounding him with love and respect. Together we prayed the Lord's Prayer, quoted the Twenty-third Psalm, and sang songs of comfort and praise. As we sang "How Great Thou Art," his golden heart stopped beating, and Dad quietly and peacefully slipped from this earth and entered through the gates of heaven. It was as if those present in the room also felt the brush of angels' wings as they ushered him away. We will never forget the bittersweet memory of that awesome experience—the day Papa went home, the day the angels came for him.

Early in my ministry, a nine-year-old child was struck with a terrible disease, Reye's syndrome, which destroyed her kidneys and left her comatose. She was rushed from Gadsden, Alabama, to a special children's hospital in Birmingham, Alabama. Little Kristi had only been saved a few months. As her pastor, I stood watch outside her room in intensive care. I was asked to go in and pray for her. The room was small, but there were two others in her room at the head of her bed dressed in white. When I came out, I mentioned the two medical staff in the room. Her parents said to me, "Pastor, there was no one else in the room." We all went back into the room, but they were gone, and so was the spirit of that little girl. Angels had come to take her home.

Take comfort if you are a Christian;
no "grim reaper" is coming for
you. Rather the hosts of heaven
will be your escort home.

ANGELS ACCOMPANIED ELIJAH HOME!

I am convinced that we do not go alone into the vale of death. Remember, angels accompanied believers home on two occasions in Scripture. One of the most spectacular occasions is found in 2 Kings 2. Elijah was at the end of his ministry and life. His apprentice, Elisha, was alongside him as they journeyed to the place where Elijah would go to be with the Lord. During their final earthly conversation with each other, the divine intersect took place. A chariot of fire with horsemen swept in and carried Elijah back into the heavenly dimension.

> And Elisha saw it, and he cried out, "My father, my father, the chariot of Israel and its horsemen!" So he saw him no more. And he took hold of his own clothes and tore them into two pieces.
> —2 KINGS 2:12

Take comfort if you are a Christian; no "grim reaper" is coming for you. Rather the hosts of heaven will be your escort home.

I have witnessed angelic ministry at the deathbed of many people across my forty-plus years as a pastor. Here are two such experiences that remain vivid in my memory.

I was a nineteen-year-old preacher in 1967 in Clanton, Alabama. I went to see a dying older pastor at the request of some of his friends. When I got there, the nurse was trying to keep him quiet.

"Don't you see him?" said the old preacher.

"No," replied the nurse, "I don't see anything!"

"There is a angel!" cried the old man.

"I see nothing," said the nurse.

He turned to me and said, "Preacher boy, look in the corner; the chariots of God have come for me."

I looked and saw a bright glow. I said to him, "I see the glow."

The nurse said to us both, "You are crazy!"

The old man shouted, "They have come for me!" He laid back and smiled and said to me, "Do you know this old song?" And he began to sing:

> O come, angel band,
> Come and around me stand;
> O bear me away on your snowy wings
> To my eternal home.[4]

The second was at Baptist Hospital in Montgomery when an elderly man lay in intensive care. He had both hands reaching upward. The nurses wanted him to relax. I went in to help, and I said, "What are you doing?"

He said to me, "I am asking these angels to take me up!"

> I looked over Jordan
> And what did I see?
> Coming for to carry me home,
> A band of angels coming after me,
> Coming for to carry me home.[5]

Addendum

CHRIST

IS *to* BE

WORSHIPED, NOT

The only One who has the right to be worshiped is the
Lord Jesus Christ. He is the King over the angels.

A CROSS THE CENTURIES FASCINATION ABOUT ANGELS
has led some into the heresy of angel worship. Though
angels are real and are to be celebrated, they are never
to be venerated. In his letter to the Colossians, Paul warns us to
avoid "worship of angels" (Colossians 2:18).

At the end of the Bible, John falls before an angel who
quickly corrects him saying, "Worship God."

And I fell at his feet to worship him. But he said to me, "See that you do not do that! I am your fellow servant, and of your brethren who have the testimony of Jesus. Worship God! For the testimony of Jesus is the spirit of prophecy."

—REVELATION 19:10

Of all the scriptures on angelic worship, Hebrews chapter 1 gives the most thorough treatment of Jesus's superiority to angels. As glorious as angels are, they aren't equal to the Son of God. Seven Old Testament passages are quoted in Hebrews 1 to emphasize the absolute superiority of Jesus above the angels.

1. "You are My Son, today I have begotten You" (Hebrews 1:5; see Psalm 2:7).

2. "I will be to Him a Father, and He shall be to Me a Son" (Hebrews 1:5; see 2 Samuel 7:14).

3. "Let all the angels of God worship Him" (Hebrews 1:6; see Psalm 97:7).

4. "Who makes His angels spirits and His ministers a flame of fire" (Hebrews 1:7; see Psalm 104:4).

5. "Your throne, O God, is forever and ever; a scepter of righteousness is the scepter of Your kingdom. You have loved righteousness and hated lawlessness; therefore God, Your God, has anointed You with the oil of gladness more than Your companions" (Hebrews 1:8–9; see Psalm 45:6–7).

6. "You, LORD, in the beginning laid the foundation of the earth, and the heavens are the work of Your hands. They will perish, but You remain; and they will all grow old like a garment; like a cloak You will fold them up, and they will be changed. But You are the same, and Your years will not fail" (Hebrews 1:10–12; see Psalm 102:25–27).

7. "Sit at My right hand, till I make Your enemies Your footstool" (Hebrews 1:13; see Psalm 110:1).

Paul chose these seven quotes no doubt to reveal Jesus's glory from His cradle to His crown. Let's take a closer look.

Though angels are real and are to be celebrated, they are never to be venerated.

THE TESTIMONY TO THE SON

The first section, Hebrews 1:5–6, begins with three Old Testament quotes. The first two refer to Christ's *first* coming and His relationship to God as His Father.

His relationship as Son

> For to which of the angels did He ever say: "You are My Son, today I have begotten You"? And again: "I will be to Him a Father, and He shall be to Me a Son"?
>
> —HEBREWS 1:5

> I will declare the decree: The LORD has said to Me,
> "You are My Son, today I have begotten You."
>
> —PSALM 2:7

Jesus was already the eternal Son of God, but He came to the earth in human form. In Luke 1:35, Mary was told that her Son would be called the Son of God. Again in Matthew 3:17, we learn more about His sonship as the Father declared, "This is My beloved Son." John the Baptist said of Him, "And I have seen and testified that this is the Son of God" (John 1:34). In Romans 1:4, we are told that Jesus is "declared to be the Son of God with power...by the resurrection from the dead."

His royalty as Son

Psalm 89:3–4 further reinforces Jesus's royalty through the prophetic covenant God made to David about his lineage and kingdom being established forever. Jesus is part of the lineage of David (Son of David) and has been established as King forever over the earth.

> I have made a covenant with My chosen, I have sworn to My servant David: "Your seed I will establish forever, and build up your throne to all generations."
>
> —PSALM 89:3–4

The second quote in Hebrews 1:5, "I will be to Him a Father, and He shall be to Me a Son," directly correlates to 2 Samuel 7:14. Second Samuel 7 is where God's covenant with David is recorded and delivered to him by Nathan the prophet. The covenant included the following promises to David: the land of Israel to belong perpetually to the people of Israel (2 Samuel 7:10),

David's house to be established and his successor to build the temple (verse 13), and David's throne to be established forever (verse 16).

As glorious as angels are, they aren't equal to the Son of God.

All these promises God has kept, including the coming of Jesus, the Son of David. Revelation 5:5 rightly describes Jesus as the "Root of David." He was both the root and offspring of David. He alone is the rightful king of Israel and of all creation.

His return as Son

> But when He again brings the firstborn into the world, He says: "Let all the angels of God worship Him."
>
> —Hebrews 1:6

> Let all be put to shame who serve carved images, who boast of idols. Worship Him, all you gods.
>
> —Psalm 97:7

Here reference is made to the *second* coming of Christ. In Jewish tradition, the firstborn inherited everything. When Jesus comes to claim His own and all the earth, the angels in heaven will bow in wonder and worship.

The name of Jesus is above any other name, including the angels. Michael is the glorious name of the angel of the Lord who watches over Israel. He is also the general of the Lord's hosts. Gabriel is the angel who served as messenger of the Lord, who carried the news of the Savior's birth to the world. But no angelic name can match the wondrous name of Jesus!

THE THRONE OF THE SON

There are two quotes in this next section of Hebrews 1 that further exalt our Lord Jesus Christ as superior to angels.

> And of the angels He says: "Who makes His angels spirits and His ministers a flame of fire." But to the Son He says: "Your throne, O God, is forever and ever; a scepter of righteousness is the scepter of Your kingdom. You have loved righteousness and hated lawlessness; therefore God, Your God, has anointed You with the oil of gladness more than Your companions."
>
> —HEBREWS 1:7–9

The angels stand before the throne

Hebrews 1:7 indicates that the angels are servants who worship before the Lord. The word *seraphim* means "burning ones." I believe they are on fire to serve the Lord. They do not sit on the throne but stand before it, ready to serve. Psalm 104:4 says, "Who makes His angels spirits, His ministers a flame of fire." This is also made clear by the angel's statement in Luke 1:19: "I am Gabriel, who stands in the presence of God."

The Son sits upon the throne

> Your throne, O God, is forever and ever; a scepter of righteousness is the scepter of Your kingdom. You love righteousness and hate wickedness; there-

fore God, Your God, has anointed You with the oil
of gladness more than Your companions.

—PSALM 45:6–7

Hebrews 1:8–9 is an echo of Psalm 45, which is a wedding
psalm. It depicts the king seated upon his throne and the bride
enthroned with him. These verses testify to the eternal nature of
our Lord's reign.

---

*No angelic name can match the
wondrous name of Jesus!*

You can see in these words the reign of joy that takes place
when Christ sits enthroned with His bride, the church. The word
gladness in the original language implies "leaping with joy." The
Lord Jesus, who was the man of sorrows, is now seen in great
rejoicing over His bride.

THE TIMELESSNESS OF THE SON

And: "You, LORD, in the beginning laid the foundation of the earth, and the heavens are the work
of Your hands. They will perish, but You remain;
and they will all grow old like a garment; like
a cloak You will fold them up, and they will be
changed. But You are the same, and Your years will
not fail."

—HEBREWS 1:10–12

> Of old You laid the foundation of the earth, and the heavens are the work of Your hands. They will perish, but You will endure; yes, they will all grow old like a garment; like a cloak You will change them, and they will be changed. But You are the same, and Your years will have no end.
>
> —PSALM 102:25–27

Psalm 102 affirms the eternal nature of the Son of God. Early in the chapter, we read of the rejection of Christ and His suffering, but the verses cited here declare His eternal and everlasting life!

The Lord is declared to be the Creator who will outlive His creation. Like a garment that is worn out, all of creation is degenerating. The Lord Jesus forever remains the same. He is eternal.

Again and again in Scripture we discover that our eternal Savior has given us eternal salvation, redemption, and inheritance. Creation may change; angels may change; but Jesus is "the same yesterday, today, and forever" (Hebrews 13:8).

The Lord Jesus is always our contemporary. He is always relevant. This truth alone gives meaning to our lives. The eternal perspective keeps us from despair when the difficult times hit.

THE TRIUMPH OF THE SON

> But to which of the angels has He ever said: "Sit at My right hand, till I make Your enemies Your footstool"? Are they not all ministering spirits sent forth to minister for those who will inherit salvation?
>
> —HEBREWS 1:13–14

> The LORD said to my Lord, "Sit at My right hand,
> till I make Your enemies Your footstool."
> —PSALM 110:1

This passage speaks of the victory of the Son of God. Psalm 110:1 is quoted, declaring that Jesus's work is finished, and now the enemy will be brought under His feet.

The Lord Jesus is seated at God's right hand, a place of honor and authority. This is the second time in this chapter that the right hand of God is mentioned. (See also Hebrews 1:3.)

Our Lord quoted this psalm as He stood before the Pharisees and challenged them in Matthew 22:41–46. When He was on trial for His life, Jesus said to Caiaphas, "Hereafter you will see the Son of Man sitting at the right hand of the Power" (Matthew 26:64). In Mark 16:19, we read, "So then, after the Lord had spoken to them, He was received up into heaven, and sat down at the right hand of God."

In the message of Pentecost, Simon Peter also quoted the same psalm, declaring Jesus to be exalted to the Father's right hand:

> Therefore being exalted to the right hand of God, and having received from the Father the promise of the Holy Spirit, He poured out this which you now see and hear. For David did not ascend into the heavens, but he says himself: "The LORD said to my Lord, 'Sit at My right hand.'"
> —ACTS 2:33–34

Paul speaks of the right hand of God as the place where Jesus "makes intercession for us" (Romans 8:34).

Three more times in Hebrews, we are told that Jesus is at the right hand of God (Hebrews 8:1; 10:12; 12:2). What is the significance of that location? It is the place of victory! With Christ's work finished on the earth, He has now gone to glory where He awaits the final triumph. First Peter 3:22 declares of Jesus, "Who has gone into heaven and is at the right hand of God, angels and authorities and powers having been make subject to Him."

Here, our triumphant Lord reigns in victory. He is Lord over the fallen angels. These forces have been defeated and are under His feet. He is Lord over the holy angels, who are servants to those He has delivered. These angels serve us, but they cannot save us. Their main job is to worship God and serve the saints of God. In Isaiah 6:3, the angels are found worshiping, crying, "Holy, holy, holy is the LORD of hosts." They served Isaiah in a ministry of discipline as they brought a coal from the altar to touch his unclean lips.

WORTHY OF WORSHIP

The only One who has the right to be worshiped is the Lord Jesus Christ. He is the King over the angels. Is He the King of your heart? Will you believe the testimony of the ages? Will you come and bow before His throne of grace? Will you lay hold of the timeless One today? Oh, that we would learn to truly worship Him and come into His presence to give Him all our honor and love!

> All hail the power of Jesus' name!
> Let angels prostrate fall;
> Bring forth the royal diadem,
> And crown Him Lord of all.

Bring forth the royal diadem,
And crown Him Lord of all.

O that with yonder sacred throng
We at His feet may fall!
We'll join the everlasting song,
And crown Him Lord of all.
We'll join the everlasting song,
And crown Him Lord of all.[1]

Notes

INTRODUCTION

1. C. H. Spurgeon, "The First Christmas Carol," sermon, Music Hall, Royal Surrey Gardens, Kennington, London, December 20, 1857, http://www.spurgeon.org/sermons/0168.htm (accessed April 2, 2009).

CHAPTER ONE
THE PRESENCE OF ANGELS

1. "The Gulf War: A Line in the Sand," Military.com, http://www.military.com/Resources/HistorySubmittedFileView?file=history_gulfwar.htm (accessed April 1, 2009).

2. Malcolm D. Grimes and Donald R. Ferguson, "Joint Publication 3–16, Joint Doctrine for Multinational Operations: 'If You Work With Friends, Bring It Along!'" *Air and Space Power Journal* 18, no. 4 (Winter 2004): 72–73, http://www.airpower.maxwell.af.mil/airchronicles/apj/apj04/win04/grimes.html (accessed April 1, 2009).

CHAPTER THREE
THE MYSTERY OF ANGELS

1. C. S. Lewis, *Miracles* (United Kingdom: Fontana, 1947).

2. Francis Collins, *The Language of God* (New York: Free Press, 2006), 124.

3. Ibid., 205.

Chapter Four
The Variety of Angels

1. Francis Brown, S. Driver, and C. Briggs, *Brown-Driver-Briggs Hebrew and English Lexicon* (n.p.: Hendrickson Publishers, 1996).

2. Billy Graham, *Angels: God's Secret Agents* (Garden City, New York: Doubleday and Company, Inc., 1975, 1995), 30.

Chapter Five
The Appearance of Angels

1. BrainyQuote.com, "Neil Armstrong Quotes," http://www.brainyquote.com/quotes/quotes/n/neilarmstr363174.html (accessed May 19, 2009).

Chapter Six
The Conflict of Angels

1. G. H. Pember, *Earth's Earliest Ages* (n.p.: Kregel Academic & Professional, 1975).

2. William Shakespeare, *Macbeth*, 1.5.51–53. References are to act, scene, and line.

Chapter Seven
Worship—Angels Around the Throne

1. John Paul Jackson, *7 Days Behind the Veil* (North Sutton, NH: Streams Publishing House, 2006), 28–29.

Chapter Eight
Destiny—Angels Among the Nations

1. Chuck Ripka, *God Out of the Box* (Lake Mary, FL: Charisma House, 2007), 102–104.

2. Ibid.

Chapter Nine
Protection—Angels on Defense

1. Bill Bright, "Guardian Angels Watching Over Us," Angel Stories and Miracles, http://www.thoughts-about-god.com/angels/bb_guardian.htm (accessed March 18, 2009).

2. Al, "Firemen and the Angels Story," Amazing Angel Stories, http://www.angelrealm.com/angels_house_fire/index.htm (accessed February 24, 2009).

3. FOXNews.com, "Caught on Camera," *FOX and Friends*, December 25, 2008, http://www.foxnews.com/video-search/m/21712317/caught_on_camera.htm (accessed February 24, 2009).

Chapter Eleven
Strength—Angels Plugged In

1. "Angel Comes to Encourage," Angel Stories and Miracles, http://www.thoughts-about-god.com/angels/surgery.htm (accessed March 12, 2009).

Chapter Twelve
Angels Obey Orders

1. Bart, "Switch Lanes Angel Story," Amazing Angel Stories, http://www.angelrealm.com/switch_lanes_story/index.htm (accessed March 13, 2009).

Chapter Thirteen
Angels Respond to Scripture

1. Eugene Merrill, *New American Commentary: Deuteronomy* (Nashville, TN: B&H Publishing Group, 1994), 434–435.

CHAPTER FOURTEEN
ANGELS ANSWER PRAYER

1. Adapted from "Prayed for God's Angels Story," Amazing Angel Stories, http://www.angelrealm.com/prayed_for_angels/index .htm (accessed March 13, 2009).

2. Gena, "Angel to the Rescue," AngelsLight: In the Light of Angels, http://www.angelslight.org/angelstory.php?id=gena (accessed March 13, 2009).

CHAPTER FIFTEEN
ANGELS MOVE ON MIRACLE GROUND

1. Terry Law, *The Truth About Angels* (Lake Mary, FL: Charisma House, 1994, 2006), 41–42.

2. Taken from the *Agape* Newsletter, Little Rock, AK, May/June, 1988, 3. This newsletter is published by Agape Church, pastored by Happy Caldwell, as related in Law, *The Truth About Angels*, 41.

3. Larry Libby, *Somewhere Angels* (Sisters, OR: Questar Publishers, 1994), 32, as related in Law, *The Truth About Angels*, 42.

4. Graham, *Angels: God's Secret Agents*, 5.

5. Victory Church of Christ, "26 Guards," http://victorychurch ofchrist.org/otherstuff.html (accessed August 10, 2009).

CHAPTER SIXTEEN
ANGELS EXECUTE GOD'S WRATH

1. Jim Bramlett, "Angels Discovered Singing End-time Song in Rural Chinese Worship Service in 1995!" Lambert Dolphin Library, http://ldolphin.org/angels296.html (accessed March 30, 2009).

Chapter Seventeen
Angels Escort Believers Home

1. Dorothy Milligan, "On Angels' Wings," *Awe* magazine (magazine no longer in print). While attempts have been made to contact author for permission to use quote, they were unsuccessful. Please forward any contact information for author to publisher of this book.

2. Charlie Carty, "My Guardian Angel Story," Amazing Angel Stories, http://www.angelrealm.com/guardian_angel_story/index .htm (accessed March 12, 2009).

3. Jim Bramlett, "Encounter #3 (Confirmed)," Lambert Dolphin Library, http://ldolphin.org/angels296.html (accessed March 31, 2009).

4. "My Latest Sun Is Sinking Fast" by Jefferson Hascall. Public domain.

5. "Swing Low, Sweet Chariot," an African American spiritual. Public domain.

Addendum
Christ to Be Worshiped, Not Angels

1. "All Hail the Power of Jesus' Name" by Edward Perronet and John Rippon. Public domain.